D0872104

Heading Nowhere in a Navy Blue Suit

and other
TALES
from the
FEMINIST REVOLUTION

edited by

SUE KEDGLEY & MARY VARNHAM

DAPHNE BRASELL ASSOCIATES PRESS

First published in 1993 by
Daphne Brasell Associates Co Ltd
306 Tinakori Road, PO Box 12 214
Thorndon, Wellington, New Zealand

ISBN 0-908896-30-1

Edited by Rachel Lawson, Whitireia Publishing
Designed by Margaret Cochran
Typeset by Wordset Enterprises Ltd
Printed by Wright & Carman Ltd, Upper Hutt

to
BARBARA & MARION
our mothers

CONTENTS

FOREWORD

WE MET 35 YEARS AGO, heading to the Roseneath Presby-
terian Sunday School in our camel-hair coats. The friendship that
began so inauspiciously has endured through the life events
typical of our middle class, post-war generation—all-girl schools,
unsatisfactory sexual relationships, various university degrees, the
writing of several books, flatting together in Dunedin, Wellington
and New York, three marriages, one divorce, late motherhood
and now (we are told) menopause.

Together and apart we became feminists. While one of us
was liberating male bastions in Auckland's Queen Street, the
other was campaigning for MacGovern in New York. In 1973 we
marched together, along with tens of thousands of other women,
down New York's Fifth Avenue behind the banners of Betty
Friedan and Gloria Steinem.

Experience radicalises. In the very early days, feminism was
an intellectual event, an ideology whose time had come. It rapidly became intensely personal, fire in the belly, a clutching at
the throat, a rage that would not go away. Mary became a pas-
sionate advocate of the feminist cause when she returned to New
Zealand at the end of the seventies to find women journalists still
having to struggle to be taken seriously. She became active in
Media Women, and later its convener for three years.

In New York at the United Nations, Sue joined the United
Nations Women's Group to try and change a system which, while
urging fairness for the world's people, kept its own female staff
firmly at the bottom of the pile. Later she returned to work for
Television New Zealand only to find it was almost identical, in its
treatment of women, to the organisation she had just left behind.
Talented and inspiring women were leaving, frustrated and disillusioned at the organisation's treatment of women staff and lack
of commitment to women's programming.

1

Activists hate to look back. It is in the nature of things that we first rail against the present and then propose a new and better way of doing things. The past is merely a distraction. Nevertheless, over various cups of coffee and in between ferrying articles to newspapers and attending city council meetings—and spurred by a feminist lecture series initiated by the Wellington YWCA in 1991— we began to talk about the movement itself—where it was heading and what (dangerous waters) it had achieved.

Had feminism done what it set out to do? Had it improved the lives of all women or just a few? Had men got the message? Had women? Would the world be different for our daughters and granddaughters?

These questions led to this book.

Most of the history we learned as we were growing up in the fifties and sixties was written by men about men. One of feminism's greatest achievements has been to make visible the invisible history of women and to see that our stories are told. Never again, we hope, will women think they were the first or only ones to feel the way they did, to experience the things they did, to ache and hunger and work for the opportunities and freedom that men take for granted.

This book is part of that process—history written by those who made it happen, to whom it happened and for whom it happened, the women of Aotearoa New Zealand.

Sue Kedgley and Mary Varnham
Wellington, August 1993

INTRODUCTION
Shifting the Goalposts

DALE SPENDER

'Not knowing our
history' was part of
the problem, write
Anne Else and Ross-
lyn Noonan in their
description of those
early days of the
women's liberation
movement of the
sixties and seventies. Not knowing our history meant that those
of us who were part of that revolution thought we were doing
something new when women—internationally—rose up and
said we would no longer stay in the place that men had put us.
We genuinely believed that we were the first women to really
understand and to state the case for women's equality and
independence.

And then when we did start to know our own history, when
through the seventies and eighties women began to generate
women's knowledge about women's conditions, and we found
that we were by no means the first feminists, we had very mixed
feelings about our status.

We were pleased to know that there had been women
from the past—from different cultures, on different continents,
and at different times—who had protested at the oppression of
women, and who had worked for reform and revolution. We
were affirmed when we found that their analysis was similar, their

arguments much the same, and that indeed, some of them had been so uppity that our demands could even look conservative in comparison. We were delighted to be able to recover our past, to claim heroines and role models, and to celebrate achievements and victories. But even as we established that for centuries women had struggled for the betterment of their sex and an end to the exploitation of women and children, most of us harboured a distressing suspicion: could it ever happen again? Were we the generation who would solve the women's problem, or—almost unthinkably— would we be but another 'wave' that would fight and campaign, make some gains, but ultimately be buried like our foremothers? Would our movement and our members disappear and remain invisible until future feminists could play their part and—in the act of documenting their antecedents—could come across our contribution? In the way we had 'discovered' for example, all those who had worked so magnificently to obtain votes for women?

Our history lesson was bitter-sweet. As woman after woman (and campaign after campaign) from the past was reclaimed, we began to detect a pernicious pattern. For no sooner did the woman—or the movement—break through the bonds of silence and achieve a measure of success, than the discrediting practice began. They were 'silly women' or 'wicked women' or 'pathetic women', who could not get a man. And as such they were mocked and maligned and their words were misrepresented, so that in a short space of time these brave women, whose only crime was to protest about oppression and to strive for social justice, were treated as outcasts.

Take Mary Wollstonecraft. After writing her brilliant analysis of women's subordination and the role that education could play in creating equality, *Vindication of the Rights of Women*, 1792, Mary Wollstonecraft was vilified. 'A hyena in petticoats,' thundered the male establishment who were incensed by the criticism of their privilege. 'A philosophic sloven,' the male intellectuals declared. And despite the huge popularity of the book and praise for the author on publication (with women all over England writing in their diaries—or to their daughters—that Mary Wollstonecraft certainly had a point), in no time at all she was being held up as a spectre to scare off the young. 'You wouldn't want to end up bitter and twisted like Mary Wollstonecraft,' the warning went to women who questioned the burdens and boundaries of their lives. And despite the fact that Mary Wollstonecraft wasn't bitter or twisted at all, just reasonably angered by men's abuse of women, it soon became the received wisdom, in feminist circles as well, that with her wildly outspoken ways Mary Wollstonecraft had put the women's movement back 100 years. The men who made the images and were in charge of the press ruled the day. So discredited was Mary Wollstonecraft that few people bothered to read the *Vindication of the Rights of Women* and to find out for themselves how responsible, reasonable and realistic was her recipe for sex equality and a just society.

And of course this isn't past history. The same thing still goes on. Every time a woman says 'I'm not a feminist' or says to me 'You don't look like a feminist', and then acknowledges that she doesn't know or read any feminist literature, it's quite obvious that she is reacting to the image of feminism as represented in the media, an image which—like its counterpart, the thin, young sex symbol—is a product of male consciousness and control.

This is why few of us as feminists were surprised by Susan Faludi's *Backlash*. Although we were shocked, of course, when all the information that she gathered was put together. We had entertained ideas about a possible conspiracy when we found that everything from 'women in the home' policies to the decision of retail stores to stop selling women's jackets in favour of 'pretty dresses' was the result of deliberate male calculations. Because every one of us who has dealt with the male controlled media knows the extent to which our meanings are distorted and our experiences ridiculed, we were not unprepared for the thesis of *Backlash*. It provided a name for many of our daily experiences, for a practice that has been going on for centuries. The issue is— what do we do about it?

This is why *Heading Nowhere in a Navy Blue Suit* makes such an important contribution. It puts the record of the past two decades straight. It shows what individual women have achieved, and what the women's movement has gained; it shows just how far removed the reality is from the rancorous railings that the movement is now over (post feminism), and that all the women involved are disgruntled or depressed with their lonely liberation.

And it is partly because we have women's presses, where

women are in charge of the images, that uncensored versions of events—such as this volume—can be published. Women can know what women have done when women can produce the meanings.

But at the same time, running through every contribution to this collection is the sense that women—and feminism—are under attack. That the gains are being eroded, the movement discredited. And the dynamism and vision that was there in the early seventies is no longer in evidence, summed up in the title of Sandra Coney's chapter, 'Why the Women's Movement Ran Out of Steam'. And while I would never want to dispute the reality of the backlash—or the danger of the present situation—I do want to make the point that there is more than reaction to feminism to reflect upon. Our recent past, like our historical past, is also bitter-sweet. In seeing both the achievements and the assaults (and the two are not unrelated) we are part of the tradition of feminism.

Of course no one expects that the women's movement would be the same 20 years on. The world has changed drastically in that period: the communications revolution, the emergence of environmental issues, the collapse of the 'alternative' to capitalism, are but a few of the consciousness transforming events that have taken place. In the light of these enormous changes, the stagnation of the women's movement would be a real worry: had it maintained its profile and agenda of the early seventies, we would now be talking about disillusionment and demise on a grand scale.

I am sure I am not alone when I express some regrets for the passing of those heady days. It was not just the novelty of protest, the affirmation of consciousness raising, the excitement of the intellectual challenge, and the sense that all was possible. It was also that the agenda was so much more simple. We were all sisters. We wanted a better world. Our cause was just. We were convinced that all we needed was to present it and our demands would be met. We—white women in the United States, Britain, Canada, New Zealand, Australia—had a charter. It was child care, reproductive rights, safety, equal wages, an end to domestic exploitation and violence. We were young, products of the sixties, citizens of expanding economies and job opportunities. We even thought it would be easy.

6

And the fact that feminism has now expanded to encompass the diversity of women's experience in different cultures and communities, that it has become more complex and more representative, is not a development we can deplore. That it has been more difficult than we imagined is testimony to our willingness to be inclusive rather than exclusive—and to our commitment to change the world.

So although we are no longer so naive as to believe that once men see the unjust nature of their ways they will readily change them, I suspect that it is because we have achieved so much that the sense of excitement seems to have dwindled. When I look back to the seventies I know that I could never have envisaged some of the material and psychological gains that we have made in that period.

To the discussion of the last 20 years of feminism, I bring a slightly different perspective from those presented in this volume. I became a feminist from intellectual conviction, with a fair share of 'housework politics' (that I did two jobs, while my husband did only one, was a wonderful lesson in injustice—and a powerful and personal impetus for change). I became a writer (editor, publisher, broadcaster) because my concern was the politics of knowledge. Having been the victim of a 'womanless' education, having been denied all information about women's past achievements, my feminist vows were that this would never happen again. That in so far as it was within my power to ensure that the knowledge about women should be transmitted from one generation to the next, I would commit my energies to this project. My priority was to counteract the backlash by helping women to voice their own experience. Initially that meant getting women into print, and getting the print into traditional educational institutions. And although it hasn't been the triumph I once envisaged, the achievements of publishing, and women's studies, are resounding success stories.

But while in relation to knowledge and power we focused on reclaiming women and changing the curriculum, the communications revolution was taking place all around us. Indeed I would now suggest that one of the reasons that women were able to break into print after five centuries of exclusion, one of the reasons that we could take charge of aspects of this book information channel that produces images and shapes cultural values, was that men were not as interested in it as they once had been. With the introduction of information technology, so many of the men moved off to manage the 'networks' of airwaves and screens, that women were able to get their foot in the door. Women got in precisely because print was no longer the primary information medium.

And while there is not the space to deal with the topic here, it needs to be recognised that many of the issues of sexual inequality have been 'transported' into the new information medium, so that in many respects feminism must—yet again—start to address these recycled problems of male dominance. With the shift from print culture to electronic came the shift from a mono-dimensional, linear, regulated and fixed reality to a pluralistic, visual, ever changing view of the world, associated with the contemporary media. And it is no coincidence that at the same time that our mind-sets have moved from the set and ordered patterns of print to the multi-dimensional and volatile patterns of the screen, that we should start to see that there is no one truth, no one movement, no simple philosophy of feminism that will serve all women in all places at all times.

We are now living in a different era from the feminism of the seventies. No doubt in future years scholars will look at the decade of the nineties and conclude that it was a period of cultural revolution. Yet just as those who lived through the 1840s in England didn't necessarily know that they were part of an industrial revolution, so too are we often oblivious to the fact that we are involved in an information revolution which has mind altering consequences.

We are the products of our culture. It is now a very different culture, in which we are called upon to set priorities and to formulate agendas. Our reality is to some degree formed by circumstances—and in the circumstances we are doing very well.

Certainly the women's movement is no longer monolithic. We have split into thousands—if not millions—of cells, with each unit establishing its local charter. And this is how it should be. For the feminist campaign of one community may not be relevant in another. This is why we have moved from 'feminism' to 'feminisms'. The diversity is a strength, not a distraction.

This is not to suggest that every woman's idea is as good as every other. While I acknowledge the full range of human rights, and the equality of human beings, I don't treat all ideas and opinions as equal. I do have criteria about reliability, responsibility, about the fullness and freedom of information and the role of self interest, which allow me to see some ideas, schools of thought, explanatory frameworks (even within feminisms) as preferable to others. I do have a framework of ethics that leads me to discount research and findings that are sexist, racist and exploitative.

We are now witnesses to an economic and information revolution: it isn't the fault of feminism that we got here and it won't help in any way to blame ourselves for the fact that we didn't predict it, or take preventive measures. Yet to deny its reality—to deny what is happening and the implications it has for women— is about as useful as denying the power of print 500 years ago. (Which is why I am critical of those who take some pride in declaring their opposition to computers and the electronic world.) For it is time for us to turn our attention to the new medium—if we don't want to be left out again.

What we have in this volume is a marvellous achievement; it is the record of an era. An enriching, affirming, fulfilling era, and one from which we should all take heart. It can also be a painful appraisal, as we recognise what has not been done and how much further there is to go. Not least with the physical realities for women. This is why I identify so much with Charmaine Pountney's account of education and the obsession of young women with body image. But I also know that such images are produced by a media that women do not control. And I know what we should be doing in the future if we want to change this pressure on women to be thin. I appreciate the achievements outlined by Allison Webber as she shows what gains women have made in the media, often at a cost. And I think Sue Kedgley's question—What's it all for, if women aim to get to the top in uncompromisingly male managerial circles?—should be another fundamental framework for the future in these days of restructuring.

Sonja Davies raises the issue of whether, in politics too, we want to play men's games, by men's rules. While no one could think the status quo was satisfactory it has to be allowed that it is a huge improvement on 100 years ago, when feminists were fighting for women's suffrage. Yes, there are problems and penalties for women in politics, but it is because there have been women in politics, and because they have been successful in subverting the agenda, that we now have better programmes for women and children. When we deplore the difficulties, let us not also forget the demands that have been met. I do not want to go back to the days when women could not own property, get a divorce, be guardians of their own children—all successes of women's political activity. We too must have a pluralist vision and hold on to the wins as well as the set-backs. Pat Rosier does this when she presents her bitter-sweet account of lesbian history; all those names, all those attainments—and all the things that still cannot be said, the individuals who still cannot be mentioned.

Dame Mira Szaszy too recounts the gains and the pains. When I read her account of her entry to the women's movement, I was humbled by the risks that it represented and the courage that it took to prioritise the treatment of women within an oppressed Maori community: .

> My speech [attacking sexism in Maori traditions] provoked a very strong reaction, even among women. The worst reaction of all came from the man who had been parading on stage at the beginning. We had quite a session after the speech. He said I was challenging customs and I said, 'Yes, I am, because I refuse to respect customs that have demonic elements in them.'

But she stood alone. Some women were even her harshest critics. It is however a sign of our times that there is no one community, and no one form of resistance. There is always diversity—what we do not want is division.

Donna Awatere Huata also tells a powerful—and empowering—story: from her entry to the women's movement in defence of her mother's right to equal pay in the sixties, to her courageous job creation enterprise of the eighties, she reveals her commitment to action. Endeavouring always to bring together her Maori and feminist ideals, she is an inspiration to all who claim justice—and pay a price.

That Fiona Kidman can tell a wonderful tale of women writers has its own wry irony. It is in the area of print that women have made their mark in New Zealand, as well as overseas. Internationally Germaine Greer, Susan Faludi and Naomi Wolf stood defiantly at the top of the *New York Times* best seller list while articles on the death of feminism and its irrelevance to modern society were being featured in many newspapers. And while there is an element of wishful thinking among those who write about the advent of post feminism, we must also note that print pre-eminence for women is only part of the story—and an increasingly diminishing part.

Mary Varnham sets out the revolution that has taken place in women's personal lives. For centuries women have had no career but marriage, no options but to be 'given' by their fathers to their husbands. Women have been controlled through marriage, motherhood, monogamy and monetary means. But the rules and retributions of the past won't work any more. Women place conditions on marriage, motherhood and domestic chores, and they have options to enter, to exit and to negotiate the terms of their commitment. Such independence would have been unthinkable to their grandmothers—and must be taken as a success story, even if the last chapter in the narrative has still not been drafted. It is no longer a case of women worrying about who will marry them, but of why they should marry at all.

Alongside the success of women writers and of 'wives' is the harsh reality of ordinary women's lives as we confront the economic upheavals of our times. The evidence that is presented by Anne Else and Rosslyn Noonan in 'Unfinished Business' and Phillida Bunkle's 'How the Level Playing Field Levelled Women' is distressing to the core. They have noted a development that we will hear much more of in the future: that of individual women in places of influence who declare their interest as feminists, but whose position and status does not seem to be sufficient to open the door for other women to enter and share the same benefits. 'Enterprise bargaining' can create divisions among women on the 'level playing field' and while women have had no say in determining the rules, they have no choice at times about going on to the field.

It is no coincidence that just as we were starting to get results and the state was beginning to open up, albeit slowly, to women, Maori and other groups, new right policies began shifting major resources out of reach, or removing them entirely from the state's domain. This is another aspect of the tradition of feminism, as the Norwegian philosopher Berit Ås has explained. Every time women get close to realising their aspirations, she says, men have a war, a revolution or a recession to justify the denial of women's rights and to oblige women to start again. In other words, men shift the goalposts when women start to play the game.

This is why Phillida Bunkle's analysis can be so energising. She labels the changes of the last decades—and she gives them women's names. In her chilling chapter she provides the words that we need to structure the reality that reflects women's experiences. The task now is to have a stake in the medium so that we can make *our* meanings accepted as the mainstream values.

Twenty years ago I implored women to set up publishing companies. Now I put my energy into urging women to set up television channels, video production units, databases and radio stations. Those who control information have the power to control society; they have the power to make sense of the world and to determine the social priorities. In this time of communication revolution we cannot allow a small group of men to exercise such power in their own interest, and with such direct advantages for their own pockets. One thing that does emerge is that the feminisation of poverty is very much with us; those who have the least are losing the most in this economic restructuring—and that means women and children.

It is not manning the barricades that I now have as a priority, but womaning the networks. That's the source of wealth, power, and influence in the twenty-first century. And it can be used for either fair or unjust purposes. For hundreds of years feminists have focused on the political moves that men have made, and have altered their agendas to meet the challenge of such change. The last 20 are no exception. But we now confront a shift in the goalposts again. Perhaps this time we should enter the field—and remove the goalposts from the game.

Heading Nowhere in a Navy Blue Suit

SUE KEDGLEY

MARTI FRIELANDER

IT WAS GERMAINE GREER WHO first sounded the alarm more than 20 years ago, back in the early, heady days of women's liberation. 'We must beware that in our quest for equality we do not simply end up with free entry into the world of the ulcer and the coronary,' she wrote in *The Female Eunuch*, which sold a record 8000 copies in three months following her controversial tour of New Zealand in 1972, and went on to become something of a bible of the women's liberation movement, as it was then called.

This would be our certain fate, she predicted, if we repeated the mistakes of the suffragettes and sought equality of opportunity within the existing, male status quo. 'Revolution ought to go much further than equal pay for equal work,' she said. 'It ought to revolutionise the conditions of work completely. ... It is not a sign of revolution,' she went on, 'when the oppressed adopt the manners of the oppressors and practise oppression on their own behalf. Nor is it a sign of revolution when women ape men or compete ... for a man's distinction in a man's world. ... We know that such women do not champion their own sex once they are in positions of power, that when they are employers they do not employ their own sex. ... Such women are like the white man's black man, they are the obligatory woman, the exceptional creature who is as good as a man and much more decorative.'

Her warning touched a nerve, and I quoted it whenever I could, for I could see, even then, how easily the road to liberation would be compromised if we were to settle simply for a piece of the male status quo.

Even so, it didn't stop me, or any of the women I knew, from wanting to enter the working world—a world women had been excluded from ever since the Industrial Revolution, when work was separated from the home. We had made occasional forays into it since then, during two world wars, and had been steadily infiltrating its hallowed ranks since the sixties, albeit in low paid, low status, traditionally 'feminine' or domestic roles.

But most middle class women hadn't spent any time in it at all. Most of our mothers had spent their lives at home instead, fulfilling their female destiny as wives and child-rearers.

Having perceived at first hand the frustration and masochism of their lives, which had been lived vicariously through husbands and children, some of us resolved not to repeat their mistakes. We would do things differently, so we set our sights on freedom and independence, not marriage and motherhood, and a chance to work, at long last, in the male working world.

Not that we intended to assimilate ourselves uncritically into that world, or content ourselves with equal access to their status quo. We were going to change and humanise the cold and ruthless world of men, if not level it entirely.

This was our goal as we left the barricades to join the workforce, and wrestled with the reality of life 'inside'. We were convinced that once we had joined male institutions in sufficient numbers they would crumble and transform under our humanising influence, and become less rigid, more co-operative, less competitive and aggressive. And once enough of us had made it to the top, the feminist revolution would have been all but accomplished.

It wasn't always easy, getting a toe-hold in the male working world. In my own case, having been suspended from one male institution (Secondary Teachers' Training College) for being a 'negative influence', and denied entry into another (Television New Zealand) because of a 'radical feminist image', I finally got my foot in the door of a large, rather unusual, albeit quintessentially male, bureaucracy in New York—the United Nations Secretariat.

On the surface, the United Nations was an extremely promising place for a woman like me to work, especially once I had inveigled myself into a tiny, fledgling outpost in the ten thousand-strong organisation, the International Women's Secretariat. The Secretariat had been set up to persuade 150 nations of the world to celebrate International Women's Year in 1975, a daunting task which I embraced enthusiastically.

As one of a handful of women who were paid to promote and publicise the women's movement around the world, I congratulated myself on having landed a job whose function was to change the status quo. 'I'm a paid revolutionary,' I foolishly informed a journalist who had come to inquire about the workings of the International Women's Year Secretariat. 'I am paid to help change this organisation.'

Slowly, however, the unpalatable reality began to sink in. The United Nations was novel in that there were people in it from every nation in the world. But in terms of being a quintessentially male bastion it was anything but novel. Its system of justice was fit for the time of Henry the Eighth. The attitudes of the majority of its predominantly male staff were about the same vintage. Women were a small, discriminated against minority within the organisation which seemed impervious to any efforts to change it.

The hypocrisy of the United Nations calling on the nations of the world to promote equality for women while denying it to women in its own ranks soon became unbearable. So a group of women decided to expose this hypocrisy and try to remove the institutional and other barriers that prevented women from advancing in the organisation. The Ad Hoc Women's Group, as it became known, was soon the most active group in the United Nations. We organised huge rallies, meetings and protest marches, enlisted the support of heavyweight feminists like Germaine Greer, Gloria Steinem, Oriana Fallaci and Betty Friedan, and even resorted to guerilla tactics such as turning up to a meeting with the Secretary General wearing black veils.

But all to no avail, it seemed. The more we protested and spotlighted the appalling discrimination against women in the United Nations, the worse our situation became.

In despair, as the years went by, some of our number gave up and left, convinced that a large male organisation was a fruitless and frustrating place for a woman, and particularly a feminist, to be. One of them, Susan Vine, left to attend the first ever feminist business course at Harvard University, run by two self-styled feminists Margaret Hennig and Anne Jardim, who subsequently wrote a bestselling book, *The Managerial Woman*, about the philosophy they espoused. Inspired by what she had learned at her feminist business course, Susan Vine arranged for Hennig and Jardim to speak to the dispirited female ranks of the United Nations Secretariat in 1977, shortly after their book had come out. Their message jolted us.

The working world, they pointed out, was created for and by men. Its rules are derived from team sports, and its structure and values resemble the discipline, control and chain of command of the military. It's a world dominated by male values, needs and perspectives, which men feel comfortable in and understand instinctively. Having played together, competed in teams together, and shared similar experiences as they were growing up, they know how to play the game, for they have been playing with miniature models of it all of their lives, especially in male sports.

When women enter the same world, they find themselves in unfamiliar territory, with no idea what the rules are or how to play the game. They are aliens in a culture designed around the needs of men. Their traditional upbringing has taught them to be 'feminine': supportive, nurturing and subservient, qualities ill suited to a world which is based around competition and aggression, where emotional involvement with people is seen to be unproductive, and the overriding goal is to win. Hennig and Jardim warned:

> Millions of women will spend an entire career life living and working in a culture whose traditions, rules and implicit codes are derived from male experience. The extent to which as women (and therefore outsiders) we can understand this culture and manage our existences within it will determine how far we can go and what costs we will have to pay.

They advised women to approach the working world, with its rules of behaviour, style of communicating and ways of relating that grew directly out of the male experience, as if it were a foreign culture. 'If we were going to a foreign country for an extended stay,' they wrote in *The Managerial Woman*,

> we would know that we came from one tradition and they from another. ... We would struggle with the language, until we sensed that we had been understood. We would try to learn what kinds of behaviour were considered polite, and what would be considered offensive. We would want to behave in ways which would win us friends. We would want to fit in and to be understood. ... We would try to identify individuals and organisations who might be helpful to us and we wouldn't hesitate to use them when they were needed. We would anticipate that we would often feel frustrated. It wouldn't surprise us if sometimes we even felt frightened and lonely. After all, we would be alone in a foreign country.

To advance in this foreign culture where the odds were stacked against them, women needed to learn what their male colleagues had imbibed on the football field and in the pub—the rules of the game. By reading books like *The Managerial Woman* and attending business courses on assertiveness training and career planning, women could learn about its culture, its male codes and, above all, how to play the game.

Playing the game, they explained, meant identifying and getting to know key people in the organisation, being seen in the right places, gaining access to information, manoeuvring oneself into strategic positions in the organisation, establishing informal networks, dressing for success in sombre suits that resembled men's, and carrying briefcases and other accoutrements that gave one an aura of competence and authority. It also meant 'learning techniques to manage your emotions and feelings', finding a style that didn't come across as too masculine or feminine, down-playing parts of your personality if you didn't want to be seen as foreign to the system, and learning to manage your personality far more effectively. In other words, modifying your personality, stamping out 'female' attitudes and behaviours, and modelling yourself on men.

The Managerial Woman quickly became a bestseller in the United States, and something of a gospel for women seeking to advance through the ranks of corporate America. Almost single-handedly, Hennig and Jardim made climbing the corporate ladder an ideologically acceptable, and even desirable, thing to do and began a fresh assault, and soon a stampede, of women into the corporate world. Their book also encouraged the establishment of feminist business colleges, new magazines like *Savvy* and *Working Woman*, and a whole new genre of books advising women how to succeed in the corporate world. Its popularity was due in large measure to the fact that it seemed to work. Where affirmative action had failed, the managerial woman philosophy seemed to succeed. When women learned the rules of the male world, and how to play the game alongside men, they finally began to climb the elusive corporate ladder.

It's hard to appreciate now how revolutionary this message sounded 15 years ago to women like myself, who were flailing around in a male maze, getting nowhere. We knew something was dreadfully wrong, but we had no idea what. After listening to Hennig and Jardim, it was suddenly obvious. We were outsiders and, worse still, feminists, in a world which instinctively rejected people who were different and did not fit in—especially people like us who had constantly, by our protests and direct action, drawn attention to our differentness and to the fact that we had no idea how to play the male game. We had, to be sure, some reservations about their theory, especially the invitation to model ourselves on men. But having tried and so manifestly failed to get anywhere by direct action and protest, some of us decided to give the theory a go.

The results were dramatic. No sooner had I abandoned my full-length peasant gear, my dress preference for many years, for the tailored suit and blouse, than my career began to take off. It was as if, in exchanging my symbol of nonconformity for a symbol of conformity, I had signalled my readiness to accept the rules and play the game. Suddenly, accelerated promotions came my way, and I found myself climbing the corporate ladder; even, eventually, being invited to help organise and co-ordinate the secret, exclusively male meetings the Secretary General held regularly with the heads of all the United Nations agencies around the world.

It was there, in the cigar and testosterone filled basement

conference rooms of this ultimate male sanctum, that Germaine Greer's warning began to echo in my ears again. As the token woman among 70 men, I was conditionally accepted—but only on their terms. If I was prepared to work 10 hour days, wear managerial woman suits, put up with cigar smoke and bad behaviour, with being treated at times like part of the furniture, and at other times like a bit of flesh they could flirt with when they needed a diversion, I could achieve a measure of acceptance. But if I wasn't prepared to make work the number one priority in my life and conform utterly to their codes of behaviour, I would be excluded from their game. I would be squeezed out of my position, to return once again to the ranks of outsider, a marginal creature men could not tolerate in their inner sanctums.

Was this, I began to wonder, the point of all our striving? To have the same opportunity as men to sacrifice our personal lives, work 80 hours a week, drop dead at 45, and otherwise trap oneself in lives that were as stressful and sterile as I perceived most of the lives of these chief executives to be?

The more I contemplated my situation, the more obvious it became that the price of embracing the managerial woman philosophy and climbing the corporate ladder would be nothing less than the crushing of my spirit and the sacrificing of my hard won independence. For the basic premise of the managerial woman philosophy, and its central flaw, is that women must change themselves, modify their personalities, and mould themselves after men if they are to succeed in the male working world. But in so doing, they will almost inevitably end up as one of Germaine Greer's 'counterfeit men', behaving like men, judging themselves by male values, cutting off their emotional circulation for 80 hours a week, and sacrificing their personal and family lives, as well as their integrity and personal power, on the altar of success.

As I looked around at the handful of women who had made it into positions of responsibility in the United Nations, I could not help noticing that they did indeed resemble the 'obligatory' women or counterfeit men Germaine Greer had warned us about—women who had not only come to resemble men but also, once they had made it to the top, found excuses not to champion their own sex.

Determined to avoid such a fate, I turned my back on the

seductions of life inside the United Nations and returned to New Zealand in 1981, only to find that, like so many American trends, the managerial woman philosophy had become well established here as well. A new breed of corporate women, or what American journalist Barbara Ehrenreich calls 'pioneer assimilationists', in smart executive suits and attaché cases, were very much to the fore. Anne Hercus, Beverley Wakem (who would later be the first woman admitted to Rotary), and politicians like Helen Clark and Ruth Richardson were becoming the new heroines and role models for a generation of New Zealand women. Studying for an MBA and dressing for success were the rage, and women parliamentarians were already throwing themselves at 'image consultants' in an attempt to transmute themselves into nonthreatening political clones. Women's professional networks were replacing seventies' style consciousness raising groups, and bookshops were overflowing with the new genre of 'how to be more like the boys' books—books that advised aspiring managerial women what to wear, how to flatter superiors, and how to suppress their emotions.

Dr Sylvia Senter, in *Women at Work, a Psychologist's Secrets to Getting Ahead in Business,* recommended:

> Traditional, feminine responses almost never work when you want to function with men as part of a business team. . . . In the business world nurturing is inappropriate, and often harmful to a woman's career. . . . You can learn to curb your nurturing instincts without feeling you are being cruel. Crying is also infantile and inappropriate in the business world. You should never do it.

In *Games Mother Never Taught Us* Betty Lehan Harragan advised:

> Women should wear jackets to give themselves a feeling of strength and control. . . . They should choose clothes that achieve a uniform look, and match the fabric and quality of male colleagues in the office. . . . In business you are dressing in a costume which should be designed to have an impact on your boss and team-mates. If your clothes don't convey the message that you are competent, able, ambitious, self confident, reliable and authoritative, nothing you say or do will overcome the negative signals emanating from your apparel.

Letitia Baldridge said in her *Complete Guide to Executive Manners:*

> Enter the bar with a briefcase or some files . . . Hold your head high,
> with a pleasant expression on your face . . . After you have ordered
> your drink, shuffle through a paper or two, to further establish
> yourself [as a businesswoman].

In *Women in Sexist Society* Roslyn Willett advised:

> Children [of mothers who are working] should be systematically
> taught, as early as possible, how to fix simple meals for themselves,
> shop, use the phone, use public transportation, read a map, and pay
> attention to written messages directed at them as well as to re-
> corded messages to other members of the family.

To my horror New Zealand women seemed to be taking all
this advice as seriously as their American sisters had. Friends of
mine were furtively reading these books, devouring their advice,
attending endless training courses, and consciously trying to
modify their appearance and their behaviour to fit the managerial
mould. In the process, many of them seemed to lose much of their
spontaneity, and in some cases their very essence.

This is an almost inevitable consequence of prolonged accommodation to the corporate world, according to Dr Harold Kellner, an
organisational consultant and clinical psychologist, who devoted
much of his career to studying the effect of 'masculinism' on
women managers. Kellner points out that women managers have
become targets of 'the most massive make over in modern history',
and have succumbed like lemmings to 'image consultants' and
other experts who specialise in advising women to remake themselves in the male mould.

> Those who wore dresses were advised . . . to buy business suits.
> Those who were quiet and reflective were advised to enrol in
> assertiveness training courses. . . . Then there was the issue of
> emotionality. How could the men around women be expected to
> put up with tears and emotional scenes in the office? So the experts
> advised women how to manage emotions in the office.

Kellner has identified three distinct stages in women's accommodation to the corporate world. In the first stage women are introduced into the masculine culture and encouraged to adapt to it. As

time passes they learn how to play the game by adapting to their environment and not challenging the values of 'masculinism'. Some do this so successfully that they move into the third stage and become isolated superstars—women in the advanced stages of accommodation who aspire to become more like men and to be liked by men, and to demonstrate their loyalty to the values of 'masculinism'.

The problem facing women who master the art of corporate accommodation, he warns, is that although it offers them some measure of business success it has a high price. In the process of accommodating, women 'integrate many male characteristics, and begin to discard the natural qualities and skills that could be useful to them as "feminine" leaders'. They also restrict their ability to develop and rely on their natural instincts—for instead of learning to trust their own feelings and use their perceptions to manage effectively, they gradually deny what they truly feel and think. They also shut down their sexuality, according to American author Camille Paglia. 'Career women in the Anglo Saxon world have desexed themselves ... when they achieve high positions ... it seems to be at the expense of their sexuality. They develop a bleached, sanitised, desexed, desensualised quality.'

Kellner's thesis bears out what American journalist Liz Roman Gallese, author of *Women Like Us*, found when she interviewed the alumni of Harvard Business School, class of '75. The women who had succeeded were those who had patterned themselves after men who had made it, and consciously chosen to 'live their lives as men in a man's world'. The majority of her sample, who were still languishing in middle management, were women who 'had not assimilated to the degree necessary to make it to the top'. Gallese concluded that the women who pulled back from total accommodation were a positive sign that women are less suited to the dog eat dog terrain of management. 'The problem may not be that women lack the capacity for businesslike detachment but that, as women, they can never entirely fit into the boyish, glad-handed corporate culture.'

Gallese's sample of Harvard women were not a particularly happy bunch, and they didn't seem to enjoy the time they spent in the male milieu of corporate management. The most successful of them, Suzanne, prided herself on being totally impersonal ('I'm not interested in my employee's personal lives. I can't do anything about the fact that somebody who works for me doesn't see his kids a lot because it's been a tough week . . . I don't see anybody I want to see either'). She was also openly resentful of women with families. Another high flyer, Phoebe, seemed to enjoy the fact that other women didn't like her, and had an almost pathological impulse to dominate others.

Like Gallese's sample, many of New Zealand's most successful managerial women don't seem to relish playing the corporate game either. Ann O'Sullivan, former Airways' corporate human resources manager, told *Management* magazine that she felt uncomfortable in the corporate environment because 'you have to shut down parts of yourself, and there is a high price to pay' for doing that. 'I really hate the degree of adaptation I've had to make to please people,' Helen Melrose, a partner in one of New Zealand's largest law firms, confessed in an interview published in the 1986 book *Head and Shoulders*. 'To be accepted in the legal profession as a woman you have to be a good girl, which means not make a fuss, not raise questions they'd rather not face, not have any personality quirks . . .' She went on to say:

> Male attitudes dominate the law profession. . . . It's a case of do things our way, and you're expected to adapt all the time. But their way is so foreign to a woman's way because it is all adversarial, patriarchal and hierarchical. . . . Male attitudes mean not acknowledging feelings, achieving at the expense of a balanced life . . . working long hours and committing yourself to the law and the firm and to work above all else.

Another high-flying corporate woman, Marcia Russell, recently walked away from a top job in TV3 because of the toll it was taking on her personal life. 'For nine months Kate had only seen this distracted and exhausted mother. I tried to take her to school each morning, but then I wouldn't be home till 7.30 and often I went back at 9.30 to work some more. I worked most weekends. I became somebody who was always at meetings, whom she couldn't phone because I was never there.' At some stage, she concluded, 'you have to decide whether you like corporate life, and . . . I have decided that I don't.'

If becoming a manager in the corporate world has taken a toll on most of the women in that world, it has extracted blood from women with children. Everyday realities include grossly inadequate parental leave, a shortage of good, affordable childcare, and the assumption by managers that women with children are insufficiently committed to their careers. 'Success [in the corporate world] is usually incompatible with motherhood,' Barbara Ehrenreich pointed out in an article in *Ms* magazine. 'It will remain so,' she added, 'as long as the fast track, with its macho camaraderie and toxic workload, remains the only track to success.' Patsy Reddy, the only woman on the Air New Zealand Board, agrees. 'Climbing the ladder demands a commitment to the job which can mean 12 hour plus working days, which women with young children often cannot meet,' she told a newspaper reporter.

Central to the male career norm, American author Arlene Rossen Cordoza points out in *Sequencing*, is the assumption that a person's career will be the highest priority in their lives. This assumption (which, she says, was developed by men with no other focus to their lives beyond work) means that women can only succeed in the working world if they can convince their employers that their career *is* the highest priority in their lives. For women with children, this meant arranging their lives the way men had done for generations, putting the demands of their career first and the needs of their families second—a requirement that creates enormous conflict for women whose families are in fact the emotional centrepiece of their lives.

Women who tried to do this and 'have it all' were dubbed 'superwomen'. By day they pretended they didn't have children, and by night they overcompensated by trying to be perfect wives and mothers. As successive superwomen collapsed under the strain of it all, the superwoman myth was punctured. But the notion that women should subordinate the needs of their families to the needs of their careers lived on. 'We need to challenge the ideology of success which insists we can have work, public esteem and success only when we are prepared to dismiss our children's needs to be with us or diminish our needs to be with them,' author Stephanie Dowrick told the *Listener*.

But even when women do arrange their lives along the lines

of men (at great personal cost), they find that most men *still* assume they are less committed to their careers than men. Equal Employment Opportunities consultant Gill Ellis says.

'Men make assumptions about whether women [with children] can meet the demands of senior positions all the time. But they don't articulate them to the women concerned. Nor do they apply them to male candidates who have young families.'

Women with home and children responsibilities are seen, consciously or not, as poor candidates for promotion, according to Gail Reichart, publisher of *Climbing Rose*, a magazine for businesswomen. Men are more likely to be able to work longer hours than women with children, and there are more rewards for men who appear to be willing to work long hours. Staying in the workplace after normal work hours allows men to keep a better 'finger on the pulse', as well as impressing the boss, she says.

WISER director and management consultant Mary O'Regan recalls a corporate manager explaining to her quite sincerely why he wouldn't promote women into management positions, even though he would like to. 'We are an aggressive company,' he explained, 'and we expect people to work long hours but women can't do this because they have to get home, cook the tea and look after the kids.'

The assumption that women with children are unable to make work the highest priority in their life is undoubtedly the reason a 1991 survey of 102 women managers by the University of Waikato's Marcia O'Driscoll found that 60 percent did not have children. It is also, no doubt, the reason a survey of 550 private and public sector managers (conducted by Ellis) found that 23 percent believed mothers were less dedicated to their work than single women; why women tend to take less time off for children these days than was previously the case; and why many women coming through management, according to Caroline Devereux, Customs and Traffic supervisor at Ford NZ, say they don't want families at all because children will interfere with their careers.

But despite the extraordinary difficulty of juggling a management career and parenting, some women say it gives them a valuable sense of perspective. 'Many of us look at our children,' Ann O'Sullivan, told *Management* magazine, 'and realise they are more important than any organisation, or we look at them and say, I'm going to manage so you are no less important than the organisation.'

Despite all the effort that has gone into penetrating the male management milieu, the hundreds of advice books that have been devoured and courses that have been attended, women have in fact achieved startlingly little.

Management magazine reports that New Zealand women's participation in management is still at a record low. Women hold 1.5 percent of public company directorships, 0.5 percent of private sector senior management positions, and make up only 7 percent of the Institute of Management managers. Although in 1993 there are six female chief executives of government departments, only 14 percent of the top management cadre of the public service, the Senior Executive Service, are women.

Far from revolutionising the ruthless world of men, as was our original intention, women's participation in, and capitulation to, management has done little to change organisational culture. Two Canadian researchers, Colwill and Erhart, set out to establish whether women's presence had changed the workplace or whether women had only been changed by the workplace. They concluded from their research that none of the predicted changes, such as a decline in organisational rigidity and competitiveness, had in fact occurred. Some of the women they interviewed felt women were more likely to be 'accepted rather than just tolerated', and more willing to 'stand up and be counted', where there were more women working in an organisation. But overall, workplaces with more women working in them had not become less competitive and aggressive. But the workplaces had changed the women working in them. Women managers were likely to be more rigid and strict than the men, and to stick to the rules more scrupulously 'because they were women, and had four men waiting to take their place'.

There is scant evidence in New Zealand, either, to suggest that the corporate world has been transformed under the humanising influence of women. If anything, it seems to have become even more cut-throat as a result of what is euphemistically called 'restructuring' or, more recently, 'rightsizing'. Even though restructuring has supposedly 'flattened' management structure, women report that they are finding the corporate world and the public service a tougher and less flexible place to work in than ever before, especially since the repeal of the Employment Equity Act in 1991. Surveys continue to report women managers complaining of hostile or at best unsupportive corporate environments, according to Gill Ellis and Jenny Wheeler in their book *Women Managers: Success on Our Own Terms*. 'Despite all the talk about different management theories,' Mary O'Regan points out, 'policy is still driven very much from the top. If anything, we seem to be heading back into more authoritarian management styles.'

As the first ever permanent head of the Ministry of Women's Affairs, O'Regan was responsible for what has been probably the boldest and most sustained attempt by a woman manager in New Zealand to change the way an organisation works. When she set up the Ministry of Women's Affairs, she insisted it would not only be an organisation which worked for women, but also a model of a way of working to which women could relate. O'Regan set up co-operative, consultative working methods, with a six member management team which made decisions collectively, a separate Maori Ministry and an extensive consultative mechanism with New Zealand women. She also attempted to eliminate the typical workplace division between private and public lives:

> If someone needed time off to care for a child, or for some other pressing reason, they would take it. It was sometimes inconvenient for us, but we were committed to this way of working. The result was an enormous work output in the Ministry, and high levels of staff commitment and job satisfaction.

Three years later, however, when O'Regan resigned, the system she set up was demolished. Her successor, Judith Aitken, disbanded the Ministry's consultative mechanisms and turned the Ministry into a policy unit operating along conventional, male lines. 'You can't put in place democratic, participatory processes in a structure which is inherently authoritarian and make it work,' O'Regan has concluded. From this perspective, what happened to the Ministry of Women's Affairs was probably inevitable. The system O'Regan set up was so alien to the conventional, hierarchical public service culture, it was like a foreign body which had to be expelled if it was not to corrupt the entire culture.

The experience of the Ministry of Women's Affairs was replicated at Television New Zealand, an organisation in which I had the misfortune to find myself when I returned to New Zealand in 1981. I joined TVNZ imagining it would be a creative, exciting place to work, very different from the byzantine bureaucracy of the United Nations. Instead I found it an overwhelmingly male environment, dominated by the infighting and politicking of intensely competitive men. The preferred management style of one of these men was to create a working environment in which all his staff hated each other. That way, he boasted, he was able to get the best out of all of them.

Within this unpleasant environment, there were some very pleasant female enclaves, such as the all-female group who produced *Today at One*. Because it was a daytime programme aimed at women, the TVNZ hierarchy tolerated this rather unconventional group of women who set up ways of working together that were collaborative, creative and non-competitive. Pamela Meekings-Stewart, who produced *Today at One*, and went on to become one of TVNZ's top documentary makers, said she got away with this and survived in TVNZ for as long as she did because she never 'played the games' or became part of the system. But in 1988, when TVNZ downsized and shed 350 of its staff, she paid the price for not having done so. Along with almost all the top women in the corporation, she was laid off. 'If you don't play their game, the system will eventually spit you out,' she says.

Mary O'Regan and Pamela Meekings-Stewart's experiences bear out the findings of Auckland University researcher Judith Pringle and Australian financial analyst Una Gold, who analysed the strategies women use to 'survive and succeed' in the male milieu of corporate management. The most common involves learning the male rules. Women following this strategy accept that male career patterns are the norm and that they must find ways to adopt to the 'right'—that is male—way if they are to succeed. According to Pringle and Gold, this is a lonely and isolating strategy which gives women a chance to be quasi men, but does little to assist other women managers. Nevertheless, they point out, it is in many ways the clearest path to the top.

Three other strategies, the superwoman strategy, the personal change strategy and the reformist strategy ('best represented by the femocrat, a combination of bureaucrat and feminist'), all accept the premise that women must play the male game in order to succeed in the system.

Only two strategies do not involve outright accommodation to the male model of management. These 'women centered' strategies set up non-threatening female niches, such as the one Meekings-Stewart established, while waiting for things to change within a male status quo. They accept female strengths, emphasise the differences between men and women, and insist that women's qualities should not be suppressed or devalued in the workplace. The weakness of these strategies is that women who opt for female niches (even niches like the one Mary O'Regan set up in the form of the Ministry of Women's Affairs) usually remain politically and económically marginal, insulated from the wider system, and therefore unable to challenge existing structures and rules. This is why, Pringle and Gold conclude, these women centered strategies are 'most likely to produce not real change, but small separate feminist enclaves which may have little direct effect on the wider society'.

According to their analysis, then, the strategies women managers have been using mean they have no real chance of changing the organisations in which they work. And this is perhaps the most disquieting aspect of the managerial woman philosophy. By its very tactics, it can only reinforce the status quo.

Even Ellis and Wheeler, who are at pains to point out that there have been *some* changes in the workforce which make it more woman-friendly (greater flexibility in working hours and a trend towards telecommuting from home), nevertheless conclude: 'we have not seen much change in New Zealand work patterns yet'.

We are unlikely to see any real change, according to O'Regan and Meekings-Stewart, until male managers accept that there is an alternative, female style of management which is different from their own. 'Things have always been done a certain way and many men can't envisage another way of doing business,' O'Regan says, 'They believe that the prevailing corporate value system, which is male, is the only one possible'. Meekings-Stewart agrees, 'We have busted our guts trying to fit in and be like men but men haven't taken even one small step to try and understand the different attributes and qualities women have to offer in the workplace.' Marilyn Waring told a women's conference in 1993, 'If we want access to their world, we are required to leave our essential womanness at the door.'

If this, then, is the reality facing women in the corporate world, that we can only succeed in it on men's terms, not our own, why on earth have we invested so much time and energy trying to make it in that world? Hennig and Jardim never asked this question. Nor do most of the *The Managerial Woman* genre of books. The odd one, like *Games Mother Never Taught You*, says the purpose of climbing the corporate ladder is not to join the boys, but to outwit them at their game (the author doesn't suggest how, however). But most of them, and the aspiring managerial women I know or read about in magazines, rarely seem to question the purpose, much less the price, of their capitulation to the male working world.

'It is impossible to sample the advice literature,' Barbara Ehrenreich concluded in her book *The Worst Years of Our Lives*, 'without beginning to wonder what, after all, is the point of all this striving. . . . Perhaps the most striking thing about the literature for and about the corporate woman is how little it has to say about the purposes, other than personal advancement, of the corporate game.' In New Zealand, Dame Silvia Cartwright, the first female High Court judge, has raised similar concerns. 'There is a sense deep within me', she told a meeting of women lawyers, 'that says of what advantage is it to women to join [the legal] profession unless its essentially male nature and attitudes can be transformed?'

Partly as a result of books like *The Managerial*, making it into the corporate world became one of the goals of the second wave of feminism, and a victory was hailed every time another woman made it to the top. Another cabinet minister! Another judge!

Another chief executive! In hindsight, however, it could be argued that, from a feminist perspective at least, climbing the corporate ladder has been a failure. As Germaine Greer prophesied, far from revolutionising the workforce, most of the women who have made it to the top have been swallowed up and sidetracked by it—largely because they have accepted equality of opportunity on men's terms, not on their own. It could also be argued that one of the reasons feminism ran out of steam in the eighties was because so many women (including activists like myself) joined the stampede into the corporate and public service world, and diverted our energies into surviving in that male milieu. Had we focused our energies instead on trying to create an alternative, female culture and different ways of working and living outside that world, the second wave of feminism may have run a very different course.

For the fact is that while the women who didn't join the stampede into the corporate world, the artists, writers and women who work from home or have set up their own businesses, have been extraordinarily successful in forging a new female culture and a new female voice, most of the 'femocrats' who stayed inside have lost their voice in the process of joining the dominant male culture. In so doing, according to American writer Anne Schaef Wilson, many of them have also lost their souls. 'In order to move up in organisations, women have often been willing to sell their souls, and to shut themselves off from their true strength and power,' she says.

Naomi Trigg, a director of Tall Poppies management consultants, says many women come to view the struggle of dealing with the corporate culture as not worth the effort. They realise they work better in a co-operative environment rather than the competitive 'get in first' atmosphere men tend to promote. She says the latest census shows that more and more women are opting out of corporate life, burned out by the effort to fit in with the demands of management structures which are unwilling or unable to value the skills they offer. Like Natasha Josefowitz's corporate woman, these women have come to realise that the risk of prolonged exposure to the corporate culture is that they will reach their destination only to discover that they have lost themselves, and their feminist goals, along the way.

I have not seen the plays in town
only the computer printouts
I have not read the latest books
only the Wall Street journal
I have not heard a bird sing this year
only the ringing of phones
I have not taken a walk anywhere
but from the parking lot to my office
I have not shared a feeling in years
but my thoughts are known to all
I have not listened to my own needs
but what I want I get
I have not shed a tear in ages
I have arrived
Is this where I was going?

Natasha Josefowitz

All the Prejudice That's Fit to Print

ALLISON WEBBER

IT HAS TAKEN ME years to understand the culture and power of the media, and the extent to which I was socialised by it. Like many feminists in the media I came to realise that we not only perpetuated ridiculous stereotypes of women but were incapable of accurately and fairly reporting the feminist movement itself. As the years have gone by I have felt other feminists' impatience towards us. Why couldn't we reflect feminism in a better light? For that matter why couldn't we reflect it at all? If we were feminists why couldn't we change things more quickly? In turn, I have felt impatient with other feminists who have not seen how crucial changing the media is to the whole feminist struggle.

I entered journalism by default—a refugee from a dismal year at university, I'd left it too late to apply for training college or physiotherapy. My father was a journalist; it was his life-long friend and colleague, Ev Falconer, who pushed me into it. Ev was the first woman ever employed in the New Zealand Press Association and had almost banged the door down to get in there. She was my first role model of a woman in the media. I can still picture her wiry frame, never without a cigarette, bent over the type-writer, a great topaz ring on her gnarled hand as it beat the hell out of the keys. Ev had always seemed a bit exotic to us as kids, with her stories of *Truth* in the twenties, radio in wartime Britain, and the *Sydney Morning Herald* in the fifties. She'd never married and yet she always seemed to have men in her life. She'd travelled, she'd interviewed famous people, and could spin a good yarn. Hers was a life-style I could definitely see myself living.

So, aged 18, incredibly naive and knowing very little about journalism or anything else, I fronted up to the editor of *The Dominion* looking for a job. He asked a few perfunctory questions and towards the end of the interview said: 'What'd you say your name was?—God you're not Ted Webber's daughter are you—he thinks *The Dominion's* an arsehole of a paper!' Whereupon he reached for the phone and rang up my father for his approval to employ me.

At that time only about three of 40 staff on *The Dominion* were women. They were mainly employed in the women's pages or in the reading room. Intelligent, highly qualified women were the backbone of newspaper proofreading, and before formal training courses cranked up this was a main route to gain entry to journalism.

One of the goals for women entering the media in those days was to avoid being relegated to the women's pages. This was inferior or 'soft' journalism where one could be buried alive under the sheer weight of jam recipes, society weddings and diplomatic cocktail parties. We certainly got the message that this was not where the action was. Looking back I feel quite appalled at the way I readily bought this stereotype. It was years later that I realised the significance of these pages and began to look at them in a new way. This was a place in the newspaper where a large chunk of women's experience could be documented and valued. It was also a place where some ground breaking work was done—much of it unsung.

My earliest memories of journalism are not of intrepid assignments and exciting interviews, but of the culture of the news room. Everyone smoked, everyone swore, and almost everyone drank. An air of sexual harassment pervaded the place, and stories of women being told their chances of advancement would improve if they slept with the chief reporter were legendary. This was where the dominant male culture reinforced its power base. Those were the days of six o'clock closing. By four everyone would rocket into action—typewriters racketing, phones ringing, people yelling. Then at five o'clock they'd file out of the news room in search of a watering hole. They were on their way to the 'Brit' to drink as much as they could before the pubs closed at six. That was the other dominant message—if you were going to make it, you had to be 'one of the boys'—and that would involve a lot of drinking.

In those days we didn't question news values or work for the advancement of women. Quite simply, the media was male, and we were all too busy surviving and desperately trying to prove ourselves to do anything about it.

It was a tough environment. Offices were, as they still are, open plan. While this created an atmosphere of chaos, action and excitement, it also created an environment for public humiliation and bullying. When I started in 1968 the Wellington Polytechnic School of Journalism had just begun—it was the only course in the country. So many people like myself entered the media without any training. We were destined for the school of hard knocks.

My first lesson in writing came from Pat Plunket who was then chief reporter:

'Miss Webber—what does this mean?' he yelled, as he read out my story, full of redundant words, to the news room.

'The woman got on the bus . . .' I quivered.

'Well, Miss Webber, if it fucking means the woman got on the bus, fucking well say so!'

On another celebrated evening, I remember the then women's editor presenting a story to the chief sub, Jack McKinnon. The pubs were then open until 10 and 'Black Jack', who was a brilliant sub, had just arrived back from his 'supper' break in the 'Brit'. He suffered from emphysema and that, combined with drinking, was fatal. He read the story and, teetering to his feet, steam almost rising from his ears, he recited it to the news room. He closed the performance with a loud guffaw: 'Well, God saw my cock off with a scissor!' Suffice to say regular exhibitions of this kind served to reinforce a very dominant set of male values.

The world we were reporting was also very male dominated.

There were no women judges, and very few women doctors, lawyers, politicians or police officers. Our contact books were full of men, interviews were nearly always with men, and when we covered meetings we were invariably the only women present apart from the tea ladies or stenographers. We were still fighting for the right to cover mainstream news stories and to gain entry into places like ships, helicopters and building sites.

Liz Brook, one of the first women photographers in New Zealand, and the first woman illustrations' editor, remembers in her early days on *The Dominion* fending off the constant assertion that she couldn't cover certain stories simply because she was a woman. In those days she was largely confined to covering the fashion scene, the races and weddings. But the bulletproof ceiling began to shatter when the section was short-staffed and there was nobody else to do the job. Di Billing, who started in radio covering the education and health rounds, went on to make a name for herself as a top industrial reporter. In hindsight she says she probably did her best work in health and education, but wasn't taken seriously by the male hierarchy until she became an industrial reporter.

The other major battle in those days was not about story content but about what we were 'allowed' to wear to work. Liz Brook remembers an edict from the editor of *The Evening Post* that women weren't to wear trousers. 'I think he thought the socialite women in town wouldn't like it. It took me several months to get permission to wear trousers. I put a notice up on the notice board and the next day everyone wore trousers.' Margie Comrie, now a lecturer at Massey University, also remembers an incident on *The Evening Post* in 1974 when she tried to cover a story on the BNZ tower in Willis Street. The building had been plagued by a series of industrial disputes, lead by the militant Boilermakers' Union. Comrie was told she couldn't do the story because she was wearing a skirt—this might excite workmen to look up her legs at her pants. The next day all the women in the office wore trousers to work.

By the time I left *The Dominion* at the end of the sixties the work scene was starting to change significantly. The Wellington Polytechnic journalism course was up and running, and graduates were moving out onto papers and radio stations all over the country. The post graduate course had started at Canterbury University, and its students were filtering through the media, bringing a new style of better educated and more thoughtful journalism.

At this time Judy Addinell came to work at *The Dominion*. She was to become a significant role model for me in the same way Ev Falconer had been. Judy, who went on to become the first woman head of the press gallery, was a classic model of an older woman journalist of the time. She was single, hard-working, and very conscientious. A former school teacher, she had a science and an arts degree. She had gained a reputation as an agricultural journalist and seemed to be twice as experienced, and twice as qualified, as most of the 'jock' journalists of the day. In a fairer world, and in a different generation, both of these women were well qualified to be editors anywhere in the country.

But even today we've only seen a handful of women rise to positions of senior management in the media. Over a decade ago Judy McGregor became a first as editor of the *Sunday News* and later went on to edit the now defunct *Auckland Star*. She was followed for a brief period by Sue McPherson who was editor of the *Auckland Star's* community newspapers. Jenny Wheeler became editor of the *Sunday Star*, and more recently Sue Carty was appointed as editor of the *Waikato Times*.

The lot of these women and the few others in media management has been hard. I remember Bev Wakem, former chief executive of Radio New Zealand, once describing it as 'being lonely out on the precipice'. Judy McGregor sums it up this way: 'I feel quite bitter that the public perception of me is that I eat rocks for lunch—that I regularly chew firewood. Standing alone as the only woman was the loneliest time of being a news manager.' Now news editor for Radio New Zealand, Di Billing looks back on years of battling for the acceptance of a female presence: 'The pattern of my career has been scepticism from older men. You can see it in their eyes. This is a middle-aged woman getting into her menopause—what the fuck is she doing telling me what to do? The only way you can cope is to repeat the message year after year, day after day.'

In the early seventies, about the same time that feminism was making its presence felt in New Zealand, I went to work for the *New Zealand Herald* in Auckland. By this time there were about

10 women in a news room of around 50. My assignments were probably typical of what most women journalists were doing then—a range of court and council reporting, social welfare, health, education and human interest stories.

Women might have been barracking for equality outside the media, but inside it there were very few women covering the traditional 'hard' rounds of politics, business, sport and police. There were also very few women sub-editors and almost no women in positions of responsibility above senior journalist.

However for many of us those days of the seventies definitely smelt of revolution. The National Organisation of Women was formed. Strong women, like Sue Kedgley, Toni Church and Mary Sinclair, started to develop a public profile. Consciousness raising groups abounded, the abortion debate heated up, people asked what homosexuals did in bed, and of course Germaine Greer came to New Zealand. She hit the headlines, not with any substantial message, but because she talked of bra-burning and said 'bullshit' in public. Her visit highlighted the essential conflict between the media and feminism.

Because at heart the media are better at isolating stories than identifying trends and issues, they didn't and still haven't come to terms with feminism as a movement which was equally as far reaching as free market economics. Instead they tended to marginalise and label leaders of the movement, and treat feminists as a vociferous, and temporary, minority group.

Stories were identified by the usual gamut of traditional male news values: firsts, bests and onlys, conflict and crisis, the deviant and demanding, the new and the different, and anything that threatened the status quo. So we began to see stories on sole mothers and suburban neurosis, on feminists and their wacky ideas, on abortion, contraception and child care. But the stories often adopted a stereotypic or defensive stance, as if the male media were looking for a chance to score points rather than understand issues.

This was the beginning of the big debate between the abortion lobby and the Society for the Protection of the Unborn Child (SPUC)—the issue that convinced me I could be part of a women's movement working for social change in society and in my profession.

In those days contraception was discussed in private but rarely in public; it was extremely difficult for unmarried women to get the pill. We used to keep lists of doctors who would prescribe it without interrogation and we were even known to share a packet between friends on risky evenings. At that time abortion wasn't legal in either New Zealand or Australia, but there was a stream of New Zealand women going to Australia and paying quite big money to have illegal abortions in the clinics of wealthy Sydney doctors. These were not the sort of stories being covered in the *New Zealand Herald* or the other daily media of the time. I can remember talking about it with a colleague who suggested that gynaecology was virtually a banned word in the *Herald*.

However, such stories were picked up by the women's press of the day, particularly *Thursday* magazine, edited by Marcia Russell. Cherry Raymond also flew the flag with her regular column in the *Woman's Weekly*, but for a while she seemed a lone voice in an otherwise traditional magazine. A prime motivation of *Thursday* was to give the *Woman's Weekly*, which had been the dominant women's magazine for years, a tune up. It also saw itself addressing a new class of liberated women, many of whom were working out-side the home. *Thursday* ran stories about women leaders, child care, abortion and contraception, the sort of topics the newspapers considered either too boring or too 'soft' to cover. It was the first mainstream populist publication to cater for a growing market of feminist readers. Now all these issues and many more are picked up by magazines like *Metro, North and South, More, Next* and the *Listener*.

Around this time Judy McGregor became editor of the *Sunday News*. One of the first things she did was engage in a massive fight with her management to drop the page three 'pin-up girl'. The pin-up was dropped—reluctantly—and Judy was warned that if the paper lost any circulation she would lose her job. While she contemplated a future as the shortest-lived editor in newspaper history she amassed a stack of positive letters from women in her top drawer. Despite the controversy it transpired that the absence of bare breasts had no impact on the paper's circulation.

In radio, too, things were starting to move. Throughout the sixties, before television gained ascendancy in the market place, the main role for women in radio had been as continuity announcers or shopping reporters. Under the tutelage of Elsie

Lloyd, and later Doreen Kelso, this extraordinary team of women, immaculately attired in hats and gloves, brought together a down home mixture of consumer reports and commercial promos from department stores and shops all over the country. They were hardworking, had the gift of the gab, and had been trained to ad lib on anything from frozen peas to french polish. They could run live commercial broadcasts, whipping up enthusiasm for any sort of fashion, furniture or food, and were, in fact, the original pioneers of talk back radio. Although almost entirely confined to the domestic arena, shopping reporting proved to be a great training ground for many women who later went into radio news and current affairs and television. Women like Judith Fyfe, Naomi Trigg, Merrin Downing and Helen McConnochie all did some time as shopping reporters.

Under the watchful eye of Jessica Wedell, radio had also led the way in developing a high class women's current affairs programme. *Feminine Viewpoint* was the original incarnation of what is now Kim Hill's domain on the *Nine to Noon* show. The programme built a reputation for its high quality interviews and some men even admitted to being devotees.

As time moved on, women's programmes and pages came to be seen as a way of ghettoizing women's issues and news. So, just as *Feminine Viewpoint* became simply *Viewpoint*, we also began to see the demise of women's pages throughout the country.

But the birth of Access Radio in 1981 went against this trend. Spearheaded by the indomitable Cindy Beavis, Access was the first media in the country to give real power to people. It demonstrated that if the media were prepared to give away power and share skills both the best and the worst of radio could be produced. Access proved to be a great training ground for people in how to use the media, and through programmes like *Womanszone* and *Lesbian Line* it brought feminists and their issues to the front line in a way we had not previously heard. Often the only media coverage visiting overseas feminists would get would be on Access.

By the mid seventies television had thrown off the mantle of subservience to its political masters and was on a wave of great expansion. Brian Edwards was setting the standard of national current affairs with *Gallery*. Inspired by reporter Dairne Shanahan, who was cutting a swathe across the country, scoring big stories for the *Gallery* boys, I set my sights on a job like hers. It wasn't until a few years later that I learned I was a freak in the system. Researchers, I was told, were supposed to have long legs, big boobs and a PhD. Their role was to get the minties on away trips.

I joined a current affairs programme called *Inquiry* in 1973. Television was still in its first phase of paternalism, but about to enter its second: there were very few women's programmes, women's issues were barely covered on mainstream programmes, and women filled the slots as presenters and continuity announcers. We certainly didn't decide on or generate content. Women had a few bit parts in locally produced dramas, and a few women, most notably Marama Martin and Relda Familton, fronted in news and current affairs programmes.

In the second phase of paternalism we saw the 'power behind the throne' syndrome. Television seemed to be busting with capable women in support roles, mainly as production assistants and researchers. While men held the glamour jobs, it seemed to me that a handful of these women actually ran the place. They were there when I started, and many of them were there when I left. They had virtually trained an entire generation of producers and directors who are now significant players in the film and television industry. But few ever broke through the barriers to produce or direct programmes in their own right.

As researchers we trained ourselves as we went along. Directors' and producers' jobs were not well-defined, so we did everything. I guess, like some of our colleagues in print and radio, we saw ourselves as women on the move. The majority of us wanted to move into reporting or production.

Through the seventies television expanded its base of local programmes. *Today At One*—a daytime current affairs show—was significant for women and the women's movement of the time. Its producer Pamela Jones (now Meekings-Stewart) had been formally trained with Canada's CBC. She remembers with some amusement being told that she wouldn't be able to do the job because of pressures 'at that time of the month'! She got on and did it anyway, and quite quickly the programme became a talking point in households across the country, breaking suburban isolation and treating female viewers at home as intelligent people worthy of regard.

The programme coincided with the second wave of feminism in New Zealand, when most of the mainstream media were treating women's libbers as extremists and social misfits. *Today At One* reported with insight the action, the debates, and the legislative reforms that came out of the movement. At election time it reported on candidates' attitudes to controversial women's issues such as abortion, matrimonial property and male violence. It also brought in-depth coverage of the national women's conferences of the decade—a feat that would be nigh on impossible to achieve in the present political climate.

The programme also had the scope and the courage to be innovative. Every week it presented *Soapbox*, a five minute programme slot where people could sound off about issues. I remember my ex-flatmate Tungia Baker doing one. She was sick of being labelled as 'the only Maori woman' to do this or that. She sat in the studio doing her knitting, telling the viewer that she was the only Maori woman in New Zealand to be wearing red witches' britches and knitting a blanket in brown shepherds wool four ply.

I also remember appearing on a panel discussion about whether women should change their names. Having recently married and not changed my name I was obviously in the anti camp. I was vastly entertained by afternoon radio host John Gordon, a bachelor then aged at least 85, telling me that if I were his wife he would regard me as a 'thoroughly impudent young woman'!

Child care was frequently discussed in all women's groups at the time. The lack of good child care facilities was a big issue for many women who wanted to work. It was also important for some of the women working on *Today At One*. Pamela Meekings-Stewart and Judith Fyfe worked right through their children's pre-school years to establish the Avalon child care centre. Ironically it didn't open until both their children had gone to school.

Di Billing, now news editor with Radio New Zealand, remembers starting work in radio news in 1975 as a sole parent with two children: 'While I was at work I went through all those years simply pretending they didn't exist. Then I'd race home to see them at night.' Another sole parent, Lee Hatherley, while working on the late night shift on National Radio, would put on a long-playing record and run home to her flat in Thorndon to check on her sick child. Billing acknowledges that women have been able to get where she has only if they haven't had any other sort of life. There are still very few women journalists who manage to combine full-time work in news and current affairs with parenting.

When I look back on my time in television in the late seventies and early eighties, I recall a time of enormous change, opportunity and expansion. We felt that we had achieved something and were definitely on the move. Across all media, women seemed to be gathering strength, numbers and influence.

In television women were moving out from back room roles and engineering small but notable changes in content. Viewers began to see stories about subjects like sexual harassment, night cleaners, the stress of motherhood, and women inside and outside the home. A growing number of programmes were primarily aimed at a female audience. Their hallmark was that they were human, useful and reflected the realities of women's lives. These were *You and Your Child* on parenting, *Its A Good Age* on issues for older viewers, *People Like Us* on emotional and spiritual subjects, and, the most famous, *Beauty and the Beast* on any dilemma, moral, practical or emotional, that its predominantly female audience wanted to write in about. *Beauty and the Beast* ran for over 2,000 episodes and pioneered discussions on child sex abuse, breast cancer, adoption, and numerous topics which are only now, a decade later, beginning to get prime time coverage on television. Panelists such as Cath Tizard, Davina Whitehouse, Louisa Crawley and Alison Holst also stood out as positive and encouraging role models for women.

At the end of 1979 I joined Media Women, a group which had been formed after the 1977 United Women's Convention. At the convention women reporters experienced both conflict and isolation as they watched their male colleagues removed from the press benches by the organising committee. In voting to have their conference covered only by women, the organisers were telling the media bosses they no longer believed that men could be objective in covering women's issues. Not only that, they didn't believe men could recognise the kind of news that would interest women. This challenged what the media believed was their freedom to cover what they wanted in the way they wanted to. If women were asking for only women to report their functions, the floodgate would be opened for other organisations to do the same.

For women journalists, such as myself, the issues were even more complex. Over the years we'd fought for access to numerous male functions and domains, and now we were being asked to collude with discrimination in support of the sisterhood. The sisterhood was also putting out a direct challenge for us to become politicised. While I wasn't personally involved with this battle, I quickly sympathised with Media Women's aims of improving the images of women presented by the media, and the status of women working in the media. Initially it provided a welcome support group for women in the media, but very soon we realised that this was just the beginning of a very long struggle.

When I became convenor of Media Women, the Equity Women's Caucus had started, aiming to improve the images of women in drama. The caucus got its initial impetus when two crudely macho local series, *Inside Straight* and *Roche*, went to air. Their minimal and demeaning parts for women led to an outcry, and Fiona Samuels, then a 23-year-old actor, brought the house down when she launched an attack on both series at an industry conference in the Wellington Town Hall.

The caucus went on to give women strength and support to push for changes in the industry. Female actors started asking for script lines to be changed and roles modified. In an episode of the series *Open House*, actor Lorae Parry, cast as a police officer, insisted on driving the car. Kate Harcourt refused to do a scene in the comedy series *Gliding On* unless the dialogue was changed to make her character less of a stereotype. However the big breakthrough came with *Marching Girls*, conceived and written by Fiona Samuels. This six-part series on the lives of young women in a marching team had a largely female cast and was a milestone in New Zealand television. It presented the ordinary lives of ordinary New Zealand women in a direct, dramatic and unglamorous way, and women loved it.

Another group that came to prominence at this time was Women Against Pornography (WAP). I can remember them coming to a Media Women annual general meeting in the early eighties, at a time when their concerns seemed quite foreign to a number of our members, who tended to support a more libertarian viewpoint. The following year we screened *Not A Love Story But A Story About Pornography* at one of our house meetings. This film made us realise that we had a great deal in common with Women Against Pornography. Media Women subsequently presented a substantial anti-pornography submission to the Ministerial Committee of Inquiry Into Pornography in 1988.

In 1979 Media Women had commissioned the first ever local study on the status, aspirations and barriers faced by women working in the media. It found that while women were usually better qualified than men, they were blocked from senior, high paying positions by both the attitudes of male bosses and the lack of child care facilities and other conditions that would enable them to resume careers in the industry after having children. The data would later be used to press, with only limited success, for equal employment opportunity policies. The research was repeated almost a decade later by the women's sub-committee of the New Zealand Journalists and Graphic Process Union (Jagpro) —the results were not found to be much better.

Media Women always found it difficult to get women who worked in disparate branches of the media together at one time. Women in different media felt they had specific issues to address, and these could often become submerged in a broader-based industry group where the concerns of women in television often tended to dominate. The women's sub-committee of Jagpro, initially called the 'ginger group', served a useful function for women in the print media. It encouraged more women to become active in Jagpro and did some useful work in politicising the union. Erin Kennedy, a stalwart of the union since the early eighties, remembers when women on *The Dominion* became so frustrated that they went to the Lizard Lounge every Thursday lunch-time to workshop stories which had been written, but had not made it into the paper. They would keep files of spiked stories and try to revamp them, putting them back into the system in another form. 'Just the fact that women went off very visibly for weekly lunches every Thursday seemed to lead to an improvement.' By this time we were all having to become smarter and more strategic in the way we worked.

Media Women also carried out research on sexism in television advertisements, and trained women to use the media more effectively. We staged awards and other activities to stir up publicity about the exclusion of important women's events and stories from news coverage, and wrote a major paper for the Royal Commission on Social Policy.

We fought vigorously against the deregulation of broadcasting, and despite losing the war managed to win a number of battles when the new Broadcasting Act 1989 was going through the select committee stages. The most notable of these was to have programming catering for the needs of women listed as a priority funding category with New Zealand on Air. The other was to extend the scope of the Broadcasting Standards Authority so it could carry out independent research.

Informally, we acted as advocates for women who suffered discrimination. In television these cases often centred on physical appearance. In one month we handled two cases which showed how arbitrary and subjective the male determined criteria were—one where a woman had been rejected for an onscreen job because she wasn't considered good-looking enough, and another where a woman was passed over because the male bosses said she was too beautiful and would distract viewers.

Another issue was the dominance of the television 'uncles'—senior male broadcasters of the ilk of Ian Johnstone, Ian Fraser and Brian Edwards. They were talented and highly skilled, and were seen to have on air authority that women simply didn't possess. But women had never been given the chance to possess it. Many talented women such as Sandra Burt, Carol de Colville and Anna Cotterell had developed strong profiles as reporters and directors, but they were never encouraged to develop to the next level. They were certainly never offered a series of their own.

In the early eighties, Television New Zealand had as many as 15 female producers on its staff, many committed to improving the images and raising the profile of women on our screens. By the nineties most of these women, caught in the 'free market' tsunami of cost cutting, de-regulation and commercialism, had resigned or been made redundant. Looking back on their long careers, many were tempted to ask what had actually been achieved. There had rarely been more than one or two women's documentaries in a year. In the entire history of New Zealand television there had only been three substantial documentary series on women—a contemporary series in 1977, a series on pioneer women made between 1983 and 1990, and a series on women's art.

In current affairs, *Close Up* had been on air for six years with a team of reporters which included many women, yet of nearly 200 programmes only 30 related to issues directly of concern to women. *Newsmakers*, with presenter Ian Fraser, had one year broken all records by interviewing 64 men and eight women. This ratio (approximately 80:20) would become increasingly familiar. The more research that has been done on gender bias in the media, the more the same figures have emerged. Research on the coverage of women's sport in the print media, carried out by Judy McGregor at Massey University last year, showed that no paper analysed devoted more than 20 percent of its total sports coverage to female sport. Another 1992 survey carried out by Lesley Ferkins showed that New Zealand women received 11.3 percent of newspaper sports coverage and 20 percent of sports television coverage. Both surveys concluded that the country had seen no significant improvement in the level of women's sports coverage over the last 12 years.

Have we made a difference? Certainly some issues are being covered far more extensively than they were. Even as I finish this essay almost a whole front page of *The Dominion* is devoted to women who have taken the top places in the New Year Honours list. We have had some major gains, especially in the area of health, where Sandra Coney and Phillida Bunkle's story 'The Unfortunate Experiment' led to the inquiry into cervical cancer treatment at National Women's Hospital, and ultimately to the official censure of a number of leading obstetricians. Thanks to the work women put in covering stories like this one and the Air New Zealand sexual harassment case, we can now see events such as these are being taken more seriously and covered more fully. We can see women columnists in action, women reporting most rounds, and an increasing number of women operating at chief reporter level. Significant progress has also been made in community radio and newspapers, where a large number of the people editing and managing papers and stations are women, probably a result of both their hard work and their readiness to be sole operators on low wages.

The nineties are shaping up to be conservative and tough. The unravelling of the welfare state and the onslaught of the so-called free market policies are having an especially harsh effect on women's lives. Benefits have been cut back and the Employment Contracts Act 1991 has eroded working conditions. Many women are struggling just to acquire basic food and shelter for themselves and their families.

A number of women journalists believe this economic climate, with its high unemployment and poverty, is making women's stories more acceptable than they have ever been. Stories which would have been seen as 'soft' and probably spiked a decade ago are now 'hot' and even sought by media bosses. It is also part of a trend, perpetuated by the *Holmes* phenomena, to 'storyise' rather than analyse issues. Instead of watching experts discuss homelessness and poverty, we talk to the homeless sole parent living in a garage or the mother of six patronising the food bank.

In direct contrast to these stories depicting women largely as victims, commercial television has enshrined an image of women as monied, fit, glamorous, sexy and nearly always in support roles. The rise of glamour duos such as Steve and Jude, Phillip and Lana, and Bob and Suzie has done little to reinforce the idea that women can do anything. In 1992 Maurice Williamson, the Minister of Broadcasting, suddenly discovered that games show female co-hosts were getting a raw deal. The following exchange which took place on *Holmes* with guests Steve Parr and Judith Dobson says it all.

> Parr: 'I'm not the host, with Jude as my assistant—we're both equal co-hosts.'
> Holmes: 'Do you get paid the same as Steve, Jude?'
> Dobson: 'No.'

With the economic downturn, over 1,000 jobs have been lost in the media. We have seen a drain of women out of journalism at all levels, with the loss most acutely felt at a middle grade or senior level where women have developed valuable skills, contacts and knowledge, and often a fiercely feminist commitment. This is certainly not new. Other than redundancy, the reasons are the same as they were a decade ago—insufficient child care provisions, lack of flexible hours, lack of opportunities for promotion and disillusionment with the media culture.

Women outnumber men entering the media by two to one, but there are still lamentably few women in management positions. This is largely owing to a media culture which has been slow to change. In many ways the situation I encountered as an 18-year-old starting at *The Dominion* persists today. It has enshrined a highly conservative, arrogant and poorly trained management which was barely appropriate in the fifties or sixties let alone the nineties. Fran Ross, health reporter on *The Dominion*, describes it as a 'mind set'. 'They've worked their way up from the bottom. They've had no management training so they carry on in the same way their managers treated them.'

Erin Kennedy says that although *The Dominion* is one of the better papers in the way it treats women, it is still very dominated by male values. 'If you look like a keen young man, and you remind Fred or Barry of what they were like when they were young, then you get a headstart over a young woman. There is still a general feeling that feminists are strident radicals who do all sorts of nasty things to people.'

But Kennedy worries most about the provinces. In Dunedin the Jagpro women's sub-committee worked for years to persuade the editor of the *Otago Daily Times* to use the honorific Ms. On the *Southland Times* they're still battling with male photographers to remove pin-up calendars from around the office walls. And, until the paper went under, male executives on the *Christchurch Star* kept a 'bonking' list, adding women to it and crossing them off when they were perceived to be unavailable.

In Radio New Zealand, however, Di Billing believes she is now seeing evidence that women's style of reporting and management is becoming more accepted and popular. What's more, it's effective. In two years, Katherine de Lore, Radio New Zealand chief reporter in Auckland, has doubled the number of stories coming out of her news room; she's had no resignations and has turned a number of journalists into award winning reporters.

Even so, attitudes in some news rooms continue to be offensive, inhibiting progress for women journalists and for women in

general. One in every two women now work in paid employment, but this is certainly not reflected in the coverage of issues
such as pay equity, child care and role-sharing. In the business
pages women get scant coverage in spite of the fact that nearly a
third of all employers in New Zealand small businesses are
women (1991 census).

In pushing for better coverage we have made little progress
by raising questions of fairness and equity. In the eighties and
early nineties we were constantly told that women were not
commercial. This makes little sense as women are the primary
purchasers of products. Usually this attitude demonstrates limited
vision and sometimes outright prejudice. While it persists, media
managers are ignoring a substantial section of their readers,
listeners and viewers.

Why the Women's Movement Ran Out of Steam

SANDRA CONEY

JENNY TUCK OF TAIHAPE HAS A happy habit of sending me poems just at the right time. When I was writing *The Menopause Industry*, struggling with the mismatch between the negative public and medical stereotype of menopause and the results of good research which said the opposite, she sent me a poem about menopause—from her own experience—confirming my tentative conviction that menopause was not the big deal for women nor the trauma the medicos, the drug companies and women's magazines would have had us believe.

My daughter tells me
there's no such thing as suburban neurosis
anymore

she should know
she works as a psychiatric nurse in a large Sydney
hospital

'Mum you never hear
of anyone suffering from suburban neurosis these days
not ever'

that's why I'm
so surprised when young Sally confides in me
'oh Jenny

I thought I was
going to faint on the way to the shops yesterday it was
so scary

I didn't know
what would happen to my little boys if I passed out in
the street'

what is this
brand new illness that's stopping Sally from going
to town

and making her
heart beat fast her hands go clammy and her throat close over
with fear?

Jenny Tuck

When I was feeling stuck on this essay, through the mail came
Jenny's poem on suburban neurosis, encapsulating one of the
themes I had been pondering myself. The women's liberation
movement of the late sixties and seventies had talked about suburban neurosis, and exposed the real situation of the supposedly
content housewife. Women trapped in their four walls, constantly
told their fulfilment lay in pleasing their husband and rearing
children, were actually depressed, lacking in self-esteem and,
according to psychiatrists, were taking tranquillisers in large
numbers. This was one of the catalysts for the women's liberation
movement.

In the eighties and nineties, suburban neurosis is no longer
talked about, indeed, the term has entirely disappeared from the
current vernacular. Does this mean that housewives have been
truly liberated from domestic serfdom, that husbands now share
the chores? Is the status of the housewife so improved that women
no longer suffer from 'the problem that has no name'? While
undoubtedly there are households where men share chores, a
plethora of research suggests that the gender balance of power in
most households and men's actual contribution to housework and
child care have altered very little in the past two decades.[1] Work
showing this has largely taken place within academic circles.

Consequently, it is inaccessible to women in the community and is rarely translated into political action.

On the contrary, home life has been glamourised and distorted in the late eighties and nineties. Advertisements on television show housewives who tyrannise their husbands for their lack of skill at the weekly shopping (the Country Blend advertisement), serenely orchestrate a hectic and manless household (the gas advertisement), and even passively excite their husbands while working in their kitchens (the Meadowlea advertisement). The middle class housewife who collects her daughter from school in an old Morris Minor combi van is depicted as the desirable object of her husband's sexual interest, her vulnerability and down home quality calling forth all his protectiveness and love. Even pregnant women, like Demi Moore, can be sexualised, turning their swollen stomachs into objects of erotic interest for money, in a new twist in the old story of pornographic objectification.

In the nineties the home is romanticised as a warm, nurturing haven from the cut and thrust competition of the marketplace, the dark violence of the streets. 'Cocooning', of course, is simply a contemporary parallel for the 'back to the home' movement of the fifties, repackaged by advertisers and marketers. For droves of women in the fifties, 'cocooning' resulted in electroconvulsive therapy, tranquilisers and antidepressants; whether it will do the same to women forty years later, we do not yet know, but women have not changed that much.

Behind the happy homemaker, the sexy suburbanite, is a quite different reality. Current unemployment means that it is hard for women to take time out of the workforce for childbearing and rearing, or if they do, it is hard to re-enter it. Discrimination against the over-40-year-olds is rife, and competition for any jobs is intense. Women have always disguised real unemployment by pretending that they 'choose' to stay home. So what happens to the women who from choice, or lack of it, stay home in the nineties? Are they immune from the psychological effects which overwhelmed their counterparts in the fifties and sixties? Or are they simply, like Jenny Tuck's Sally, invisible, lacking a voice. Without an organised women's movement to articulate their problems and to provide a political context in which individual women can make their demands on the home front, 'the problem that has no name' has become nameless again, whatever the reality of domestic life.

Despite the perception that women's liberationists were out to destroy family life and belittle housewives, the movement, in the early years at least, provided the only organised effort to alter the situation of suburban women. It was feminists who talked about housewives' depression, elevated the status of housework by defining it as 'work', wrote about 'the politics of housework', started community centres, organised workshops, and provided a sustained resistance to policies which would have locked women in the home. It was also feminists who established refuges for battered wives, talked about rape within marriage, supported single mothers, opposed adoption, and made films about the position of women in marriage. It was feminists who insisted on the personhood of wives and mothers, and told women they need not apologise for being 'just a housewife'.

In 1972 when the government introduced legislation to provide an accident compensation scheme for all New Zealanders—all except housewives, that is—feminists lobbied to have them included, however partially this was achieved. This issue provides a kind of litmus test for where the movement has since gone. In 1992 when the National government redesigned the accident compensation scheme, entirely disenfranchising women in the home in the process, there was barely a peep from the women's movement. There was organised opposition to specific sections of the legislation from feminist interest groups—such as those working with sexually abused women—but no effective voice for the thousands of women in the home who were about to become second class citizens all over again. The movement was silent because there is no movement—only isolated groups working on specific issues. The local women's liberation groups with a broad platform of aims have all but vanished.

In the nineties it is hardly possible to talk of a 'movement', as the term implies breadth, activity and some commonality of purpose. The women's movement in New Zealand exists only in pockets, as rape crisis centres, refuges, groups against pornography, and women's centres. The only major national or umbrella organisations are either co-ordinating bodies for a network of like-minded service groups—such as the refuge network—or they are traditional women's groups which pre-date the womens liberation movement—such as the National Council of Women (founded 1896, revived 1917), YWCA (the first branch founded 1878 in Dunedin) and Maori Women's Welfare League (founded 1951). In the absence of any more radical alternative, these more conservative mainstream groups usually represent the voice of New Zealand women at a national and public level.

These groups represent a moderate line on most issues, and adopt moderate tactics, primarily making submissions and other representations to decision-makers. Slow progress is usually the outcome of such strategies. The growing power of the media to influence public policies is not exploited by these groups, who usually do not favour public actions which risk media ridicule and condemnation.

Apart from this, reaction and action is spasmodic, unsystematic, and reliant on some women, somewhere, being moved to do something. There is no plan, no overall strategy, no feminist spokeswomen, no person or persons in charge. Much energy goes into services for women who are victims of male violence and male power, and little into challenging male power at a structural level, in the parliamentary system, the media, the family or marriage, or into exposing and remedying the disadvantaged position of women in the economic system.

The Clerical Workers' Union collapsed after the passage of the Employment Contracts Act 1991. Without national awards, equal pay can no longer be sustained and many women workers are in small workplaces whose employment contracts need not even be registered. Young Maori women have some of the highest unemployment rates at nearly 50 percent.[2] On all these issues there is virtual silence.

There is no broad women's movement to articulate the concerns of women, to demand attention and action. In many areas, the individual women who speak out are not part of a movement, and they lack the support and systems of accountablilty which would make them more effective. The media approaches known people for comment, in the absence of any other clearly identified group who could comment. As a feminist with a public profile who is relatively easy to access, I am constantly asked to comment on everything from beauty contests, to Madonna, to women smoking. If it is not an issue I am working on, I try to refer the media to a person or group who is, but I am sometimes stumped because apart from the single issue groups, such as Women Against Pornography or Help, there are no broadly feminist groups who could comment.

Enormous gains have been made for women, but so much more might have been gained, and so much of what we had gained might have been saved, had there been a powerful, articulate movement which was a political force to be taken seriously.

Yes, there are enormous numbers of women whose lives have benefited from feminism—even if they don't or won't acknowledge it—and there are very many women who could count themselves feminists, but whose area of action and influence is limited to their own immediate circle of work and community.

And there are very many young women who deny that feminism is necessary for them: they have choice, can do what they want. In fact they embrace the trappings of female subservience: the high heels, short skirts and wonder bras. It's all simply what they choose to do. They regard feminists and feminism as passé, a seventies fad which has very little to do with them. As for being another generation of fighters in the cause—it does not occur to them.

The aim of this essay is to explore what happened to the movement and why. If I draw conclusions they will be tentative. The picture is complex, and this is being written virtually in a vacuum. There is an absence of debate—an exception being Camille Guy and Alison Jones' paper 'Radical feminism in New Zealand: From Piha to Newtown' in *Feminist Voices* published in 1992. There is an absence even of a forum where this might take place.

One of the effects of a lack of an organised movement to provide a commentary and critique of change is the uncontrolled nature of the change that then does take place. Women's liberation aims which have been realised often have a different effect on women from what was intended. For instance, feminists argued for day care so that women with children might have the ability to work if they chose or needed to. They encountered fierce opposition on the grounds that children would be damaged by separation from their mothers, and that woman's 'place' was in the home. Today these objections are not advanced, but despite the existence of both working mothers and day care we have not won on this issue. Day care is expensive rather than free as demanded in women's liberation manifestos, and so is accessible only to middle class women. It is not even tax deductible, and there is an unknown amount of unsupervised backyard child care going on. More than that, women now often feel they have to justify not staying in the paid workforce when they have small children, and must paradoxically argue for their right to stay at home. Then again, although mothers are now able to work without attracting the same level of criticism, their responsibilities to children must be invisible to the workplace. The workplace has not changed to accommodate women's role as mothers; instead women are expected to participate as if they had no children at all.

But these pieces of unfinished business are not even contested in the nineties. The women's liberation movement that demanded free, 24 hour child care, and that the workplace acknowledge women's role as mothers, is silent. Somewhere, somehow, the fire went out of the movement's belly. It became torpid, jellyfish-like, its form and parameters amorphous and ill-defined, its nerve centre burned out. Maybe a better metaphor would be a star exploding, its separate pieces whirled off into other galaxies beyond reach, its brightness diminished, its fierce, searing intensity gone.

I would source the point at which the movement was inexorably set on the path of self-destruction as the 1978 Radical Feminist Caucus held at Piha, near Auckland. This event was not the cause, but it was the final catalyst. Shortly afterwards, *Broadsheet* was rent by what went down in feminist lore as 'The Split'. The lesbian members of the collective resigned, leaving the heterosexual members including myself to carry on, which we did.

When, the next year, the biennial United Women's Convention was held in Hamilton at the Waikato University, the forces that had been so destructive at Piha reached their full expression. An open forum on the university campus green was hijacked by one group who would not let any other women use the microphone. Heterosexual women were expelled from lesbian workshops, lesbians who provided entertainment were criticised for performing for heterosexual women. Buildings were graffitied with crude slogans—the damage justified on the basis that they were male property. Finally, the police were called after threats had been made against some of the conference organisers. It was the death-knell of the women's liberation movement and it was not possible to come together in such a way again. A national gathering on health was held in 1983, but this time it was the politics of race which split people.

I remember during the same period being part of a group which organised a meeting for Pakeha women to look at our obligations under the Treaty of Waitangi. I and quite a few others had by this time moved into the anti-racist movement, as it was then known. For me, it was initially a more comfortable place to be. Quite apart from the justice of the cause, there was ironically more recognition of the needs of women like myself who were mothers than in the women's movement, and a sense of idealism and of welcome that was a change from the perpetual attacks which had become the hallmarks of the feminist movement. (This was not to last, but that is another story.)

The meeting for Pakeha women was held at the Ellen Melville Hall and there was a very good turnout. The purpose was to look at how Pakeha women might support the forthcoming Waitangi protests. It was clear from the beginning that no such constructive outcome could emerge. As soon as our appointed chairperson rose to welcome women and spoke some words in Maori, she was challenged by other Pakeha women on her right to speak words in Maori. She was accused of appropriating the language. Another speaker was challenged over the use of the word 'Maoridom' which was deemed unacceptable. These were only the first of such 'challenges', the effect being to create an atmosphere where only the very brave or the very foolish dared speak. Proper debate was impossible under these circumstances.

The 'challenge' had by this time become virtually an art form within the feminist movement. The rationale was that after years of being nice girls, we should express our anger, and speak our minds. In reality this resulted in a form of politically sanctioned bullying or 'trashing' as the Americans called it.

I remember sitting at this event with a sinking heart, realising that our hoped for mobilisation of women was doomed to be buried under the weight of political point scoring, and jockeying for the most politically correct position. The whole procedure had a ritualised and ceremonial quality, and reminded me, as I detached myself sufficiently to regard the scene with some objectivity, like a political chess game.

The coup de grace for the meeting was reached when a small group of Maori women arrived. They did not seat themselves in the hall, but went into the kitchen, where they were visible but apart, like a set of avenging angels waiting to strike. When we broke into small groups, they distributed themselves among the groups. The women in mine told us that any tactics short of going all the way (arrest and prison), were so pathetically timid as to be unacceptable and evidence that we were trying to protect the comfort of our white privilege. In other small groups, women were told the most acceptable form of support was money. When we moved back into the main group, a call for a collection of money for the 'cause' resulted in a large sum of money being collected, a measure of the level of guilt and submission felt by many in the audience. Looking on the bright side, I saw this as at least something positive to come out of a stillborn movement of Pakeha women.

This kind of experience had become so common in the late seventies and early eighties, that women gave up on the feminist movement. It was simply too frustrating, too painful, too confusing. Any kind of action was impossible while the movement simply tore itself apart from within. Ironically, it was not men—'the enemy' as some were so fond of calling them—who did it, but women who did it to each other. I simply got a stomach ulcer and chronic back pain and carried on.

Women had been told the women's movement was about 'sisterhood', support, women-identified women—instead it destroyed women and ate them up. Feminists talked about the women's community but it was riddled with factions, 'in groups', and 'out groups' and hierarchies. We were told that women had different values from men, but those values appeared not to include democracy, fair play and honesty. Women were meant to be better, kinder, more nurturing people than harsh, aggressive, power hungry men. And yet women indulged in purges, coups, ostracisation, and brutal confrontations, which often included a special manipulativeness that they had learned to get their way in a man's world.

Women who retreated from the women's movement either 'went home', which might involve literally that or concentrating on a career or some other pursuit. Or they went into other movements—the unions, the peace movement, the environment, anti-racism—where they could still work to improve the world, but without having to be part of the women's movement. Groups which had a specific service focus, such as rape crisis, sexual abuse counselling or refuges, survived because they had specific tasks to carry out and were less prone (although not immune) to ideological splits. Some level of government funding also helped stabilise these groups. Other groups, such as the Women's National Abortion Action Campaign (WONAAC), survived because of the long-term involvement of a few very committed women, who once again were focused on a single issue.

The movement changed over the late seventies and early eighties from a network of women's liberation groups with wide aims, which came together periodically at caucuses and workshops (for instance, Hamilton 1975, Wainouiomata 1976, Auckland 1976, Christchurch 1977, Piha 1978), to a fragmented conglomeration of groups which might have no contact with each other. It is not really possible to describe this as a movement.

I have already said that Piha was the catalyst, but not the cause—so what was the cause? To answer that question, I need to go back. For the seeds of the movement's failure were built into it.

It is no accident that the demise of the movement can be pinpointed to the late seventies. For the whole of the seventies the dominant focus of the women's movement was abortion. 'A woman's right to choose' and 'abortion on demand' were central platforms of the movement from its earliest days. In 1970 abortion was difficult to access, and dangerous. Women were forced to go to backstreet abortionists, or clandestinely into a private hospital where the techniques—such as hysterotomy (a kind of abortion by caesarian section)—were invasive and compromised a woman's future fertility. Most doctors and Family Planning clinics would not give contraception to single women, and yet the so-called 'sexual revolution' encouraged women to have sexual intercourse before marriage.

Women's control of their bodies was an urgent issue and demanded attention from the movement. The threat to women was from outside, from governments, legislators, the church, anti-abortion groups and conservative moralists of one sort or another. It provided an external focus, a rallying point for women of many different persuasions. Kaye Goodger and other socialist women spearheaded much of the early action. Women from Auckland Women's Liberation—radical feminists—went to work as counsellors at the Auckland Medical Aid Centre, popularly known as the Remuera Abortion Clinic. Radical women formed WONAAC—while more moderate women worked through the Abortion Law Reform Association of New Zealand, and later through groups such as Co-Action and Repeal.

In 1976 at a National Abortion Conference held in Auckland, women as diverse as National MP Marilyn Waring, Labour MP Whetu Tirikatene-Sullivan, and health activist Sarah Calvert spoke from the platform. The issue of abortion united feminists of many shades against common enemies—those who would impose compulsory motherhood on women. Women reporting on the National Radical Feminist Caucus held in Auckland in 1976 complained that very little had been achieved, but one commented that it was 'significant that in the absence of any real attempt to thrash out our political differences, the only issue on which positive plans were made was the abortion campaign'.[3]

But by the late seventies the abortion campaign was winding down, not because of victory, but because of defeat. Although abortion was more available than it had been in the sixties, either because structures were set up for getting women to Australia or because the Auckland Medical Aid Centre found ways of operating within the law, all the protest activity had only resulted in one of the most repressive pieces of abortion legislation in the western world. Writing of this campaign Viv Porzsolt said:

> A major defeat has been the abortion legislation. With the polls showing a majority of New Zealanders supporting a woman's right to choose to terminate her pregnancy, the women's movement was not able to mobilise that opinion into a significant political force.

> The reformist feminists were not interested in getting masses of women onto the streets while 'radical' feminists were not interested in the tedious boring work of organising that would have been required. Spontaneous personal action, at all costs—in this case at the cost of all New Zealand women.[4]

Porzsolt was quite right in her analysis. The women's liberation movement was unable to move past small zap actions—chaining off Auckland's Victoria Street, for instance, was an understandable enough act of frustration and anger, but a powerless and futile gesture nevertheless.

By this time, organising had not only become difficult, it was a dirty word. 'I felt on reading and re-reading the last few issues,' said a *Broadsheet* reader, 'that if I heard/read the word "organise" once more I'd scream.'[5]

The defeat of one of the movement's central aims—a woman's right to choose—did not lead to soul-searching or debate about effective tactics and organisation, but it did have a psychological effect. Faced with a world that was cruel and hard to change (the abortion defeat was only one of many), women turned inwards onto the movement, and onto each other. The 'enemy out there' was big and powerful—within the movement people were simply human sized, and far less formidable targets.

The women's liberation movement had been founded on the notion of 'sisterhood'. Women were a 'class' with common interests. The simplicity of this idea masked the complexities of the real differences between women—differences based on economic class, sexuality, race, and whether a mother or not a mother. These differences involved differing experiences of oppression, and sometimes different attitudes towards the 'enemy'—men. Because the impetus from the movement had initially come from young, white, middle class women, the goals of the movement reflected their world view and were not adequate to cover all women, yet there was an assumption that they were. By the mid-seventies, these goals needed renegotiating to be more embracing, but this process did not occur. Instead there were power struggles, and offensive and defensive positions were taken. The new 'politic', if it was to emerge, would not incorporate new ideas with the old, but supercede them. Integral to this struggle was a process of attempting to discredit the old politic, and those who subscribed to it, to enable it to be replaced with the new.

The ideological and structural basis of the movement encouraged this to happen. The structureless method preferred by the movement did not provide sufficient controls to prevent personal attacks, and the ideology provided a justification for them. Structurelessness failed the movement in many ways.

The small cell group structure was adequate for the first heady days, when small groups of women needed to talk—'consciousness raise'—and take zap actions which highlighted the issues, gained publicity, and told other women a movement existed. To encourage participation and to allow all women to have a voice, the ethos of these groups was that they should be leaderless, informal, and make decisions by consensus.

In reaction to the grandstanding of males in left wing groups, and the support roles usually played by women, members were to be encouraged by sharing roles and tasks, having rotating or multiple spokespersons, and discouraging any kind of specialisation. Anyone who came to the group had an equal role to play with other members, no matter what their length of involvement or demonstrated commitment. There were no membership fees, enrolment forms, or applications for membership.

It must be noted that the problems this was meant to solve were sometimes fictional in the New Zealand context. The major influence in the women's liberation movement was American. The British feminist movement tended to be socialist and Marxist; the American movement had grown out of the civil rights' movement and university based left wing politics. In these organisations women had been treated as coffee makers, typists and easy lays. The structural model of the women's liberation movement with its emphasis on egalitarianism was meant to prevent this kind of elitism. But there was no parallel for this experience in New Zealand.

Most of the women who joined the movement became political de novo, and while some groups were university based, most were not. The left wing women who formed groups, such as Women for Equality, were not motivated by a desire to escape their men. Indeed, men were members of many early groups and left as women gained strength rather than through any overt rancour. *Broadsheet* had men in the early stages, who produced illustrations and covers, and pasted up copy. Contrast this with later stages when there were even objections to using photographs *taken by* men, even though they were of women.

The structural model of the early groups was borrowed, and even in their country of origin there were reservations about their effectiveness from an early date. Joreen wrote her seminal 'The Tyranny of Structurelessness' in 1972,[5] bemoaning the fact that structurelessness had become 'a goddess in its own right'. She said that while this model worked for consciousness raising, it didn't work for an action role, but that groups appeared unable or unwilling to change their structures to suit their new tasks. So, she said, the movement was 'stuck at an elementary stage of development'. Joreen pointed out that structurelessness was in any case a myth; it simply allowed other less identifiable power structures to operate. Friendship networks, or informal elites, could then control groups, making it difficult for other women to get in.

At early feminist caucuses within New Zealand, the dichotomy of structure/structurelessness was discussed, but with no resolution, and ironically the very structurelessness of most caucuses paralysed progress. Looking back over the old *Broadsheets* it is surprising how often the structure of the movement was discussed. It was a pressing issue, and many realised that without some form of structure the movement could not actually move. But no one could agree what that structure should be.

The Radical Feminist Caucus in Wainouiomata in 1975 was called to try and work out long-term political goals for the women's movement, but came unstuck over differences in political orientation and the inability of the structure to allow constructive grappling over those differences. Writing in *Broadsheet* Sally Casswell gave a good description of the way a structureless gathering failed to cope where there were clashes of women with different goals: on the one hand a group of 'women-oriented women' wishing to simply spend time together in an all-female environment, sharing 'warmth and strength', and on the other, the feminists who wanted 'direct political action'. According to Casswell, a group of *Broadsheet* and other women who had been meeting in an Activists' workshop at the caucus, frustrated at the lack of progress, structured the situation on Sunday to ensure that those topics on which agreement had been reached in the Activists workshop were all considered and supported by the main meeting. . . . The way in which a few articulate and strong women dominated the meeting aroused a lot of hostility among some of the other women present . . . The 'cultural feminists' were obviously disturbed by behaviour so alien to the feelings engendered by their workshop experiences and their general pro-woman nurturant line. Those 'political feminists' who had attended the socialist workshop were justifiably mistrustful of the obvious manipulation of the situation by a self-determined elite. . . . The main question to be discussed by radical feminists, must surely be whether the ends achieved at the Caucus justified the means employed. Maybe they did. I personally shared the frustrations felt by the *Broadsheet* women. It is an impossible task to sit by and watch the wheels of patriarchal capitalism grind inexorably on, passing yet more legislation designed to reinforce sexist attitudes, and still accept the rate at which the Women's Movement, crab-like, moves. But to adopt male ways to achieve one's ends, however laudable those aims might be, is also to do the feminist movement a disservice.[7]

This account is interesting because it shows how easily one group which had caucused separately and which contained powerful individuals could take over the larger group, because there were no controls to prevent this happening. It was simply achieved by force of personality or informal leadership. The *Broadsheet* group (of which I was one) wanted to set directions for the movement, and progress was too slow. As with most feminist caucuses, there was only a weekend in which to achieve this, but the movement had no structural way of setting goals and ensuring these could be met.

At Piha in 1978, there were similar occurrences, except that this time it was the lesbian group who caucused separately, to the extent of excluding heterosexual women from their sleeping space, and who were numerically in the majority for probably the first time at any caucus.

There were other problems with the structureless methods adopted by the women's liberation movement. Unmanaged discussion and consensus could become a way of bludgeoning people into agreement. Ironically, while it was designed to encourage participation, less articulate women could not operate within it. At the fiery Piha caucus, many women felt totally silenced. Over and

65

over again at meetings, I have heard it plaintively asked why some women remain silent. Ironically, structurelessness is actually intimidating to less confident women, and allows more vocal women to dominate. Being one of those woman, I have often perversely been made to feel this is some fault in me, and that I should hold back and silence myself. Individual women are located as the problem, rather than the structure analysed and altered so that more can participate. People with energy and ability were left in a difficult position. They were held down to the level of the group; their talents never allowed to fully flower. In the effort to equalise women, the movement actually had a leveling effect.

I found that my writing took off once I stopped writing for *Broadsheet*. The kind of column I have been writing since 1986 for *The Dominion Sunday Times* (now *The Sunday Times*), and for which I constantly get positive feedback from women as a much-needed public expression of feminist views, I could never have written for *Broadsheet*. At that time, a regular column by one person was not acceptable. This would have been seen as 'personality politics', attracting attention to the individual rather than the group. The use of the word 'I' when writing was not acceptable; neither was 'women'. Instead, both should be replaced by the collective 'we', reinforcing our global sisterhood. The kind of strictures I found controlling were not bluntly articulated, or written down as rules. They existed in one's own head. Actions were weighed up against the current code of political correctitude. A personal censor, like a tiny internal voice, told you what you could and could not do.

At a national meeting of women's health groups I attended in February 1992 many of the drawbacks in structurelessness were glaringly apparent. But now women glibly talk about consensus as being 'a woman's way of doings things', and argue against more formal structures as being 'the male way'. Most of these women have never debated the issue of structure, have never read Joreen. Structurelessness has become a dogma, a hallmark of the feminist 'method' which is completely accepted. At this meeting, no one knew how to deal with the failure to reach consensus on some issues. A vote was sometimes resorted to, without going into any of the procedures which would normally preceed a vote, such as the formulation of a resolution, an invitation for people to speak for and against it, and a decision to vote only when all arguments had been heard.

Another issue discussed by Joreen back in 1972 was the so-called 'star system'. The rejection of leaders or spokespeople for groups was designed to prevent individuals becoming too powerful and to encourage all women to be leaders, but it actually had the opposite effect. The media and the public were then able to select people who stood out for some reason without the movement having very much control over who they were. 'If we don't have our own leaders,' said Charlotte Bunch, 'government women or women who write books will be seen as the leaders. It's inevitable because they are public figures.'[8] These 'stars', as the movement labelled them, were not accountable to the movement, and because they were often attacked by other women, tended to withdraw even further and become even less accountable.

In New Zealand, during the late seventies, Marilyn Waring, as a young prominent feminist, came to represent in the public mind the face of radical feminism in New Zealand. It always seemed inappropriate to me that a woman in a right wing government should be seen as a movement leader, but the leadership vacuum within the movement itself allowed this to happen. In the nineties, book writers such as Susan Faludi and Camille Paglia have been designated the luminaries of the movement. They are lauded on television and attract audiences of women hungry for the feminist inspiration they will never get from movement leaders, because they are not allowed to exist.

Writing about the anti-leadership line of the movement, Carol Hanisch of the American radical feminist group Redstockings said:

> Who it came from, I'm not entirely sure. . . . No leadership, no spokeswomen, no votes, action by consensus. It sounded so good. But what started out as a utopian vision has ended in a nightmare.

The 'no leadership line,' she writes,

> was a denial that any leadership or the necessity for it even existed. Based on the dogma of exact equality among women, it denied the reality that some people are the first to dare and do, to provide clarity and insight, to teach others, to speak for themselves and for others who are not yet speaking for themselves directly. It further

denied that some people actually know more because of the kind and combination of experiences in their lives and therefore have more to teach.

Finally, she says, it stopped radical feminists from taking their politics to the masses of women.[9]

The lack of large organisational structures in the movement allowed groups which did organise nationally—usually more moderate groups—to control by default the response on women's issues. These groups usually possess a clear manifesto, and statement of aims, something which early women's liberation groups worked on and published, but which later groups neglected. The formulation of manifestos is a valuable political process for clarifying aims and providing a clear statement for intending members of groups of the basis on which they come in. Without this, the way is left open for takeovers by cliques who disagree with the direction of the group, or wish to use some assets of the group for their own ends.

The other key factor in the demise of the women's movement lay in its ideological framework. Just as the commitment to structurelessness became dogmatic and rigid, so did the tendency to 'correct' ideological lines.

The dominant ideology in the early years was for equality for women to be reached through equalising women's opportunities and pay in the marketplace (towards which the provision of free child care was a platform), control of fertility (safe contraception and free, safe abortion), reform of the structure of the family and marriage, an end to sex role stereotyping of children (freeing women from the exclusive burden of household work, and men from the breadwinning role), and an end to the depiction of women as sex objects. Women for Equality, another group of which I was a member, also demanded the right to work, alternatives to monogamy, and children's liberation.[10] The key words were 'liberation'—a positive and relatively joyful word denoting freedom—and the articulation of 'demands' which would lead to 'the improvement of the position of women in our society'.[11] The tone of the movement was active, assertive and confident.

Maybe such optimist and ebulliance could never have lasted. But as time went on the tone of the movement became more obsessed with the most depressing aspects of women's position.

Violence against women—rape, wife beating and later incest—was raised by the women's movement. These were important and critical issues, but they contributed to a change in the public face of the movement—away from women demanding liberation towards women endlessly spelling out what beasts men are and dwelling on the victimisation of women. They contributed to a change in perspective from seeing men as human beings who held structural power from which they benefited (but who therefore could have it taken away or shared) to women as victims of men's evil natures. The early manifestos of both the groups I belonged to did not even point the finger at men: structural change was called for which would 'improve the quality of life of men, women and children in New Zealand'.[12]

The political position of biological determinism defined men as irretrievably misogynous and oppressive to women. American Jewish lesbian Andrea Dworkin who heard this position articulated at a meeting, described it with distaste:

> men are biologically inferior to women; male violence is a biological inevitability; to eliminate it, one must eliminate the species/race itself (means stated this particular evening: developing parthenogenesis as a viable reproductive reality); in eliminating the biologically inferior species/race Man, the new *Ubermensch* Womon (prophetically foreshadowed by the lesbian separatist herself) will have the earthly dominion that is her true biological destiny ... [the] incipient SuperWomon will not do anything to 'encourage' women to 'collaborate' with men—no abortion clinics or battered woman sanctuaries will come from her. After all, she has to conserve her 'energy' which must not be dissipated keeping 'weaker' women alive through reform measures.[13]

This kind of thinking lay behind alienating slogans such as 'All men are rapists.' It not only precluded any support from men, but bewildered and repelled non-movement women. It was not possible to reform or change men, and not desirable to have equality with them. In fact, the logical outcome of such a theory was that men should be avoided as much as possible.

This thinking set the scene for the politics of separatism or cultural feminism. Writers such as Mary Daly (*Gyn/ecology*) and Elizabeth Gould Davis (*The First Sex*) rewrote history, creating a mythical prehistoric dream-time when women lived in harmonious women-only communities, reproducing themselves by partheno-genesis. Presiding over this happy world was the Mother Goddess, cast in the form of a Mesopotamian fertility cult figure, pregnant and large breasted. Cultural feminism defined the ancient matriar-chies as a time when women were ascendant and the progression of history since that time as steadily downhill. This reversed the analy-sis of theorists such as Simone de Beauvoir in *The Second Sex*, who saw women's recent history as one of continual struggle and gradual progress.

The American feminist Brooke described cultural feminism as 'the chador or women's liberation' and described how it

> evolved into spirituality and goddess-worshipping cults, disruptive 'dyketactics' groups and—more peacefully—academic cultural femi-nism, the main activity of which seems to be reading novels by women. Cultural feminism is an ideology. It is *not* the same thing as women's art. Artists aren't automatically cultural feminists any more than other women.[14]

The purpose of cultural feminism was to create an enclave within the dominant culture, a separate women's community where women lived with each other, frequented women's clubs and restaurants, and patronised (or 'matronised') women's businesses. As much as possible men had to be kept out of this world. Women had to try to live as if men didn't exist. Liberation was not to be sought materially, but psychologically, through a new interior and domestic world.

Thus work on one's personal life became political work. It was not necessary to impact on the world; the correctitude of one's lifestyle became the main arbiter in the political pecking order. Thus how one looked, dressed, socialised and lived became matters of comment and criticism within the 'women's community'. Any-thing which could be deemed to be giving a nod to the dominant culture was out of bounds. Someone like me, who wore lipstick and skirts, sometimes even painted my nails, couldn't hope to measure up. There was a good deal of puritanism in the new politics. Women felt obliged to stop shaving their legs, even if they then hated looking at them. Only a certain sort of jewellery—one earring, feathers, feminist symbols on leather strings—was alright. The pleasure that could come from playing with dress and appearance had subsumed into a monolithic ideal of feminist attractiveness.

This retreat from the real world would have been fair enough for the individuals who chose and attempted it, but it had consequences for other women in the movement. Separatism was morally superior. It was seen as a purer way of life, a way of 'living your politics' that was not available to women like me—mothers of sons, who loved men. Separatism was not just a political position, but a moral position occupying the high ground. Those of us who fucked men, and worse still enjoyed it, were seen as selling out. At the Piha congress, we were no longer even seen as consorting with 'the enemy', but as 'the enemy' itself.

This particular view may have only been held by an extreme few; nevertheless, it was a powerful denial of oneself to face. I was often angered at the highly negative views of men expressed in front of my son, then entering his teen years. Even my orgasms, I was told, were a myth, the result of my confusion about my anatomy, or perhaps I was faking them to please men (see Anne Koedt 'The Myth of the Vaginal Orgasm').[15] The movement had broken ground by allowing women to talk freely about their sexual satisfactions and dissatisfactions. Suddenly I found that my own experiences of sexual and erotic pleasure could not be true— the clitoris was the only site of sexual enjoyment and for that you didn't need a cock. On the *Broadsheet* collective, the question of paying lesbians more wages than me was seriously discussed, to make up for the fact that as a sole mother I paid less tax. This, apparently, was my 'heterosexual privilege'. Ironically, all the while the movement was raging with bitter attacks, my greatest sources of comfort and support were my family, my male child and my male lover. The place that I always felt totally safe was in his arms.

The movement of the late seventies and early eighties disintegrated over the politics of vanguardism, complicated by the politics of race. Pecking orders and hierarchies of oppression developed and one was a more or less valid person according to where one stood on them. As New Zealand feminist Alison Jones expressed it: 'The more oppressed were to be listened to; not because we needed to understand what they had to say, but because their membership of certain suffering social categories gave them the moral edge.'[16] The theories which supported this were non-negotiable. Certain disadvantages in life placed one's politics beyond debate. They were 'derived from personal experiences' and therefore not open to argument.[17]

That this was allowed to happen can be sourced to the original doctrines of the women's liberation movement. One of the key slogans of the movement had been 'the personal is political'. This was designed to encapsulate the premise that what happened to an individual woman was often part of the condition of being a woman. Her experience was not just personal, but shared. Consciousness raising was designed to draw this out. The slogan also contained the meaning that women's personal lives, particularly their domestic and love lives with men, were politically structured. Who did the housework was a poltical issue.

But the slogan was also interpreted to mean that the more 'oppressed' the person, the more innately and automatically 'political' the person was. It meant too that personal experience and emotional (gut) feeling often overrode rational thought and objective analysis, which was accorded a lower status. Analysis and debate were male ways of doing things. It was easy to dismiss someone's ideas by accusing them of behaving 'in a male way' or having 'man in the head'. 'The elevation of personal consciousness,' wrote Viv Porszolt in 1982,

> means objective analyses of processes which by definition are outside our experience are regarded as alienating, male, authoritarian. We talk about my reality and your reality as if there is no such thing as an objective reality, a reality that we need to investigate rationally in order to gain *power* over it. We treat our own experience as both a final product and a final reality.

This led feminists to fail to see the *causes* of experiences—usually large scale social structures and relationships extended in time and space.[18]

Porzsolt argued for a mass movement, but felt that it could not happen because of a lack of will and because of the internal dynamics of the feminist movement. Another writer to *Broadsheet* summed up the women's movement as 'a bitching club [from] which the greater number of us are barred'.

This is not true of the women's movement any longer. The

old divisions have softened somewhat; old protagonists now greet each other in the street, like the old soldiers of all sides who recently gathered at Gallipoli or Al Alamein. But the movement that was started so bravely, and with such high hopes, over 20 years ago is gone. It is difficult to see how it could be mobilised again except on an entirely different basis, learning from past mistakes. It is probably impossible for the old soldiers to do this, because of bad histories and because they are still somewhat wedded to the old ideas.

Is there any chance younger women would kick things along? For this to happen they would have to believe that a movement had something to offer them, that it would not be puritanical and that it would not deny them sources of pleasure—such as friendships and relationships with men—as politically incorrect. The material conditions would also need to exist to spur another wave of action. The progress for women made during the last 20 years means there is not quite the sense of urgency there once was.

I began this essay by contemplating how much things were the same for women in the nineties as they were in 1972. I want to finish by stressing how profoundly they have changed. Whatever the state of the movement, women's lives have changed, both materially and psychologically. This is not the place to list all the unfinished business, the areas of their lives where women still suffer—suffice to say they do exist.

But the demise of the women's movement leaves for me a feeling of profound disappointment, a sense of waste. I hope if another generation of women pick up the torch, they will at least learn from our mistakes.

References

1   Ruth Habgood, 'On His terms: Gender and the Politics of Domestic Life'. In *Feminist Voices*, Rosemary Du Plessis (ed), Oxford University Press, Auckland, 1992, pp 165–168

2   Anne Horsfield and Miriama Evans, *Maori Women in the Economy*. Ministry of Women's Affairs, 1988, p. 55

3   *Broadsheet* June 1976, p 14

4   *Broadsheet* July/August 1982, p 48

5   *Broadsheet* September 1978, p 6

6   Joreen, 'The Tyranny of Structurelessness'. In *Radical Feminism*, Anne Koedt, Ellen Levine and Anita Rapone (eds), Quadrangle, New York, 1973, pp 285–299

7   *Broadsheet* January 1976, pp 7–8

8   *Broadsheet* June 1979, p 19

9   Carol Hanisch, 'The Liberal Takeover of Women's Liberation'. In *Feminist Revolution*, Redstockings, New York, 1975, pp 128–129

10 Women for Equality manifesto, circa 1971

11 Auckland Women's Liberation manifesto, circa 1971

12 Auckland Women's Liberation manifesto

13 *Broadsheet* September 1979, p 28

14 *Broadsheet* May 1982, p 39

15 Anne Koedt, 'The Myth of the Vaginal Orgasm'. In *Radical Feminism*, Anne Koedt, Ellen Levine and Anita Rapone (eds), Quadrangle, New York, 1973, pp 198–207

16 Alison Jones 'Is Madonna a Feminist Folk Hero? Is Ruth Richardson a Woman?: Postmodern Feminism and Dilemmas of Difference'. *Sites*, Spring 1991, p 90

17 *Broadsheet* September 1978, p 6

18 *Broadsheet* July/August 1982, p 47

19 *Broadsheet* March 1983, p 3

Opening My Mouth

DAME MIRA SZASZY

IN 1973 I WAS INVITED TO SPEAK at the first United Women's Convention. I spoke in response to an article about Maori women in *Broadsheet*. In my opinion the *Broadsheet* writers had misrepresented the traditional history of Maori women, and had imposed their own analysis of what was happening to us and how we felt about ourselves. I spoke about what I knew to be the real situation of Maori women. At the end I said we were like the crippled member of the children's group who followed the Pied Piper of Hamlin. We were being left behind. Pakeha women were being led to the mountaintop while we were still picking ourselves up to start walking. As I saw it, we were still trying to survive.

I was a lone voice then, speaking out the way I did, and I remained a lone voice right up until the eighties. But because I was so involved in the Maori Women's Welfare League and in working with Maori women, nobody challenged what I said. They accepted me in a sense as a leader who was speaking on their behalf. They trusted me to express what was happening to them.

That speech was my first involvement in the women's movement. As the only girl in a family of six, I had had to fend for myself and battle with my brothers and I became quite a tomboy.

But it was my experience as a welfare officer in Auckland in the fifties which first made me conscious of women's concerns. And when the women's liberation movement began in the seventies I immediately related to what our women like Donna Awatere and Ngahuia Te Awekotuku were saying. These were issues I had been conscious of before. I hadn't marched about them, but I had dealt with them.

I was one of the first Maori women to be a social worker, and the youngest in our group. I worked in Auckland at a time when Maori were migrating there, and I saw at first hand what Maori women were going through in their homes. I was disturbed by their husbands' attitudes, and the way they were oppressed. When men came home from the pub they would often beat their wives and threaten them not to tell anyone about it. The women themselves were so trapped in their lifestyles they didn't see the oppression.

My particular area of concern was housing, and I tried to get families, and especially husbands, to put money aside from their salaries to buy a house. In those days Maori had to deposit £3,000 before they could begin the process of acquiring a house. But most husbands wouldn't agree to put the money aside from their wages. They suggested it come from the family benefit, which was all the pocket money women had to spend. I could relate their situation to my early childhood, particularly their poverty, and I sympathised with them a great deal. I was very conscious of the unfairness of it and that feeling stayed with me.

While I was working as a welfare officer, the Maori Women's Welfare League was set up by the controller of the Maori Social Welfare Organisation, Rangi Royal, and his female staff. Rangi recognised that Maori culture forbade women to stand up and speak on marae, so women had no opportunity to express themselves and their needs within the larger Maori world. Maori women themselves were also becoming conscious of their needs and status and wanted an organisation that was truly Maori. At the time there were Health Leagues in the Rotorua area which catered for the health needs of Maori children. Rangi Royal recognised the value of their work and wanted to extend them, but the district nurse who had set them up refused to allow the word Maori to be added to their name. The Prime Minister and Minister of Maori

Affairs were enlisted to try to persuade the nurse to change the name but she refused. So Rangi set up a separate Maori women's organisation. The female officers of the Maori Social Welfare Organisation established branches of the Maori Women's Welfare League within their welfare regions.

The Maori Women's Welfare League became the first national body to speak on Maori issues on behalf of all Maori. It handled everything for about 10 years before the men realised what was happening. When they became aware that women were usurping their authority, they set up the New Zealand Maori Council. Before then we had Maori leaders from all over New Zealand bringing their women to the League conferences and supporting them, commenting only when they were asked to do so. They never interfered with the proceedings of the League in those early days.

The League spread very quickly. It was the first experience we had of assembling together nationally as Maori women. It dealt with the same issues I had come across as a welfare officer, such as housing and women's health. An early example was when the Ministry of Maori Affairs said they were not building houses for Maori because Maori were not applying for them. So Auckland members collected 500 applications to prove there was a need. The League was also the first Maori organisation to ask for assistance to send our children to secondary schools, and it built health centres in Hokianga and Te Puia. Women who became pregnant in Hokianga had been very isolated. They had big families, and couldn't leave them to travel a long distance to hospital. But with the new health centres, they had time to rest and prepare for birth, and could get to the hospital quickly when the time came. The League also fought the considerable prejudice against employing Maori people, especially from banks who said Maori couldn't be trusted with money. It was involved in almost every aspect of Maori life, from birth onwards.

I had been interested in women's liberation from the time it was first publicly debated. My perspective was one of human rights and the Declaration of Human Rights. Within the League, though, the issue of equality wasn't dealt with explicitly. Members accepted my various pronouncements but they didn't see it as a big issue.

77

I was the first woman in recent times to raise publicly the issue of speaking rights of Maori women on marae. Maori women leaders such as Whetu Tirikatene-Sullivan did not support me, at least openly. Those who did were the younger women such as Ripeka Evans. I remember sitting on one side of the stage at a Labour party function and somebody suggesting I stand up and speak. One of the men from my tribal area said, 'No, a woman can't stand and speak'—even though this was a hall and not a marae. Afterwards a man told me the story of his mother at Waitangi back in the forties, who was condemned for standing up to speak on the marae. She raised her skirts at them and was almost hissed to her grave as a result. I said to him, 'Are you suggesting that's what I do now?'

There was some antipathy from Maori men towards the early Maori women activists, but I was not personally attacked until 1983 when I gave a speech on sexism to the conference of the Maori Women's Welfare League. I suddenly got a strong reaction from Maori men, and even from my own tribe.

Up until then I had felt racial issues needed to be dealt with first. I had held myself back from becoming public on the status of Maori women for 20 years. I decided to speak out, finally, because it was my swansong. The following year I was going to retire and go home to find myself. I had performed all my life as a collective being and I needed to find out who Mira was, where my inner being came from. I had reached the stage where I had to come out and say how I felt regardless of the reactions. I've said to men who criticised me for doing it that I will continue to open my mouth even unto my grave. In fact I will have my mouth open even in my casket about these issues—but perhaps my inner being will seek other dimensions!

I spoke very strongly in 1983, partly because I was angry about the way a man had stood up at the opening of the conference, parading sexist innuendos and saying things like, 'I don't want to come under the petticoats of women.' My speech provoked a very strong reaction, even among women. The worst reaction of all came from the man who had been parading on stage at the beginning. We had quite a session after the speech. He said I was challenging Maori customs and I said, 'Yes, I am, because I refuse to respect customs that have demonic elements in them.' I asked him, 'What is your reason for not allowing women to stand on the marae to speak?' He came out with all sorts of things, even saying we would invoke black magic if we did. I said I would not be subjected to those practices and I was not afraid of those sorts of things. Women did not come forward and support me. I felt absolutely isolated, even from my own people. My cousin was there and I asked him afterwards if he was annoyed with me. He responded by saying, 'Blood is thicker than water. Don't ask me any more than that. You're my relative so I can't condemn you totally.'

After my speech in 1983 I moved away from the Maori Women's Welfare League. I didn't want to disturb the president and her status by interfering. To me the League had retrogressed somewhat. I resented the invitations to so many men to speak at our conferences. In my time in the seventies, one man at the opening was quite adequate. Presidents had begun to take the conferences to marae, and to do that is to invite a completely different procedure, because the marae is a place controlled by men and you cannot change that. You cannot tell people on a marae who should welcome them to their area. It's their decision. I had also come to see the procedures of the League as outmoded for approaching the government and acting quickly. Conferences were held once a year. Resolutions were passed to the appropriate ministers who took their time, and it was the next conference before we got a reaction and acted accordingly. When something happens you must react quickly or the moment passes. I wanted to move into a group that was immediately proactive and direct.

In the 10 years since I had spoken at the first United Women's Convention, I had established links with the younger generation of Maori women, women like Ripeka Evans, Donna Awatere, Leanne Farach, Aroha Henare and others. The younger women were highly energetic and ready to put their minds to an issue. I said to them, 'You've done your radical thing out there and we all appreciate it. We agree with your basic principles, even if we don't always agree with your strategies. Now you have to think of the next step. You cannot continue to stand out there and never move. Try and get into the areas of decision-making. Get jobs.' I think I even talked about changing their style of dress so they would get positions when they were interviewed.

A lot did get themselves into positions where they could influence decision-making. Ripeka was appointed to the Maori Development Commission. She worked as Maori cultural advisor for Television New Zealand and has been involved in a group pushing for more Maori broadcasting. She was also a consultant for the recent referendum on electoral reform. Ngahiti Faulkner went into the Human Rights Commission and then the Ministry of Agriculture and Fisheries. Donna, of course, went off into private business and set up Ihi Consultants. These women have been effective to a degree but I don't think they have been successful in Maori women's terms, other than for themselves.

I was not linked to Donna or Ngahuia Te Awekotuku in the early days. They belonged to another generation and were coming from another perspective. I sympathised with them and the reasons they were marching, but I wasn't on the same wavelength. I couldn't be. I can't expect to live the lives of younger people. I've just finished reading Ngahuia's book, *Mana Wahine Maori* and, although I accept her right to it, I still feel somewhat alien from her lifestyle. It's an abyss between us I guess. I felt these women were expressing their own views and feelings rather than speaking on behalf of Maori women. The women's liberation movement seemed somewhat alien to most Maori women, even though they were conscious of the basic issues of discrimination and the sexism of Maori men.

Ngahuia has written that Maori women protect their men and cover for their weaknesses. We fear to do anything else because to expose them would be to bring shame on the whanau. That's true, we cover up a lot. I found this when I established a house for incest survivors. The extended family covered up; wives especially covered up for their husbands. The covering up has slowed down the outward expression by many women of their own experiences. They're trapped in the culture.

Many Maori women have gone into positions of power, in government departments, particularly in the Department of Social Welfare. When I was on the Social Welfare Commission, they complained to me that although they held higher positions than our men within those departments, the men continued to oppress them. They wouldn't recognise them as managers. When it came to Maori protocol, the women were pushed aside and the men insisted, although they were junior, that they stand and make the speech of welcome and so on. That hasn't changed. The women are looking for somebody else in the Maori world to make the changes on their behalf. They're crying over it. But who is prepared to make that change?

I was a member of the advisory group on setting up the Ministry of Women's Affairs in 1984. We put a submission on Maori women to the Minister, deciding this time we were not going to be left behind—we'd get moving and get in as early as possible. It's hard to say whether the Minister, Ann Hercus, supported the aspirations of Maori women. Maybe she supported some but not all. As a member of the advisory group I initially had faith in her, but as time went on that faith diminished. I felt she was giving the Maori Women's Welfare League slightly different information from what we were sharing in the advisory group.

There was a degree of resentment on the part of the League towards the establishment of the group who presented the submission to the Ministry of Women's Affairs. Later I discovered they felt the League should have been the one to undertake the exercise and they blamed me for working with another group. But of course it was up to them to take whatever initiative they wanted. Nobody stopped them from doing that. As I was no longer president or even on the executive, I couldn't persuade them to do what I wanted.

We wrote the submission in one weekend. Donna Awatere came to one meeting. Dr Paparangi Reid and others were there, but only the core stayed to do the hard work. Three or four women worked through the night to put together the package to present to the Minister the next day. We called for the inclusion in the Ministry of a secretariat for Maori women. We hoped it would employ Maori women, make all the decisions about Maori women's issues, and we also hoped the secretariat would get Maori women to argue for their rights to be equal within the Maori world. We claimed that because the female presence was so strong in Maori legends this could be used as a starting point to change the thinking of different tribal groups, to make them aware of the status of Maori women in traditional and ancient times, the beginning of life as Maori knew it.

Of all the things we wrote in the submission, though, the right of Maori women to speak on marae was the one that wasn't followed through. The secretariat, Te Ohu Whakatupu, decided government policy was their role and, I believe, side-stepped this issue. I was personally disappointed but I didn't want to interfere too much. We had appointed a director of the secretariat and I didn't want to undermine her position. Also the relationships within the Ministry of Women's Affairs were fragile and the organisation itself was under scrutiny by the government. The staff had to work out a way of progressing together, meeting the requirements of government, and looking into policies on the urgent issues such as housing and health. But I dreamed of hearing they had taken up the issue of speaking rights. It didn't happen and became obvious it wasn't going to. When the director of Te Ohu Whakatupu went out to Maori gatherings she took a male to speak for her on marae.

I cannot see women getting equality on the marae in my time. That's why I say my mouth will be open even unto my grave. A lot of it has to do with the women themselves and their attitudes about their men. To a degree they accept violence. Some are angry but can't do anything about it. Some do something but then forgive very quickly. A judge who helped us with our house for incest survivors told us there were a lot of women going to court all beaten and battered. He would ask them what they wanted to do, and by and large they would go home. Black and blue, they would still go home. They grow up thinking there's no way out. They are prepared to suffer so they can still have their husbands with them. They're prepared to suffer to have—what? Perhaps companionship. Perhaps social acceptance. But I think there is something else. There is a need somewhere inside those women that means they can't bring themselves to be alone.

The statistics we produced in the submission to the Minister of Women's Affairs in 1984 about the situation of Maori women were terrible, but I believe they wouldn't be too different today. Feminism has not improved the lives of Maori women from an economic point of view. I doubt it has even improved their lives psychologically. But I've been removed from this in my retirement and also in the work that I do. You might say I've gone fishing. In my isolated place way up in the north, I can speak on the marae. I don't usurp the position of the elders at the beginning of the welcome, but often they ask me to speak afterwards. If I want to say something I get up. Even at a tangi I would get up and speak.

But my position is unusual. In general men try to keep the power within the male sector of the community. I interpret it as basic insecurity. Our men do not have power within the wider society so they cling to their power within their own community. Maori men who have achieved positions of power, such as members of parliament and cabinet ministers, are more liberal as individuals, but in practice they don't rock the boat. Some have married Pakeha women and have no place to speak of the status of Maori women. I have had a go at a lot of them about their thinking. You might ask why I married a Pakeha. The Maori world, because of our status and small population, has become a close group. For me anyway all Maori men are my brothers and I couldn't bring myself to marry my brother.

I said in 1983 that only when Maori women reached old age and were seen as no longer a threat to male domination, were they generally free from discrimination within Maori society, at least outside the marae forum. This is still true. Their age allows them to say things that really are listened to, even if they are not accepted. If more older Maori women were to speak out about the rights of women they might have some effect. Women like Eva Rickard and Nganeko Minhinnick (who is fighting for the Manukau Harbour) are very brave in lots of ways, but not brave enough to break through the culture. Whina Cooper hasn't. Whaia McClutchie was the only one. And she did it because among the east coast tribes it's been normal for women to be leaders—they have been allowed to speak—because of their line of descent. But even there some of the men are now starting to argue against women having that status.

I ask myself whether women have to be a collective group to push those issues. Or can individuals change the way things are? They need to be very strong. As one gets older, one becomes more assertive and inclined to open one's mouth more frequently, and without fear of challenges. I am fearless now because I'm not beholden to anybody. If I want to talk about Pakeha, I will talk about Pakeha. If I want to talk about Maori, I will talk about Maori. I am a free agent. But that's not true for a lot of women who are still dependent on their husbands for income and support.

83

There is now a new generation of Maori women, younger than those I worked with, who are going through the experiences I had in the beginning. They seem to be holding back, accepting the culture, not pushing for equality. Perhaps they are trying not to challenge the men, giving them time to change. It could be that they're just being introduced to things Maori and so they are embracing the entire culture. Maori women are reluctant to speak out about their status in Maori society. Some are experiencing oppression in their own lives; others are comfortable with their lifestyle and don't see the need to go public for the sake of those who are suffering. But they are suffering very much—more now than ever before because of the economic situation. Maori women are in a very bad way.

People have asked me if I believe there is a unique form of Maori feminism. In a sense I'm loathe to use the word feminism—it seems alien. But I can't find an equivalent in Maori. If I did I would have to go back to the goddesses in Maori legend. Why were so many females present in creation mythology? The dignity of the female in Maori culture may come from those origins. That's the closest I can get to what is called feminism, but I would like to find another word in the Maori world.

When I think about the Maori Women's Welfare League, it seems to me there was a spirit there. It had to do with what the women did, and how we went about doing it. My fear is that that spirit will be lost because the League's activities seem to be changing as they move into a very materialistic, monetarist world. In those early days our women did things without thinking about being paid. If we thought about money, it was money to help the education of the children, to develop the marae, to improve the dining rooms, to establish health centres. That spirit, which emerged in an organisation for women, is the nearest I can get to a Maori definition of feminism. Women worked without self for the good of the whole. I cannot give it a name.

How the Level Playing Field
Levelled Women

PHILLIDA BUNKLE

IN 1988 I SPOKE AT THE WOMEN'S Studies Association conference in Nelson about the policies of the new right and the devastating effect they were having on women. By then Women's Studies conferences were the only formal, large scale feminist gatherings. Feminism had been re-born in the relatively affluent seventies when it was possible to travel and to organise, but by the late eighties women were suffering in disproportion to men from losses in employment and cuts to social services, and few had the money or time to travel to major events.

In my speech I said that we were ruled by ideologues of the new right, which was really the born-again old right of nineteenth century competitive individualism. The view of the idealogues was that individuals were naturally selfish and always sought to maximise their own self-interest. Men were not human beings but 'egotistical rational utility maximisers'. Only individuals counted. There was no public or social good. The wondrous efficiency of the market was threatened by any sort of collectivity, be it unions, the welfare state, the churches or the possum skin producers' board.

The only legitimate collectivity was the family, which was perceived as 'natural'.

In 1987 and 1988 I had travelled the country raising money for legal representation at the Cartwright inquiry for co-researcher Sandra Coney and myself, so that we could speak for the women who had suffered under Dr Herbert Green's treatment of cervical cancer patients at National Women's Hospital. I had experienced firsthand the rage and dejection of women. It had become clear to me that, despite Prime Minister David Lange's attempt in December 1987 to rein in the Rogernomes through resisting the regressive flat tax, there was in society a growing sense of betrayal. The employment situation was dismal. The new inequality was penalising the weakest; young, brown and female people were paying a disproportionate price.

The new system was said to be 'efficient', but for whom? Job losses were celebrated by the Business Roundtable as increasing productivity, because they meant the remaining workers had to do more work. But the division of society into the over-employed, the non-employed and the semi-employed, who occupied a growing world of casualised work for short-term contracts, looked to many of us like an inefficient distribution of society's tasks and resources.

After my speech I unwittingly became the visible face of feminist resistance. I was deluged with invitations to speak. Some were from feminist groups. Many, to my surprise, came from elsewhere—Women's Division of Federated Farmers, business and professional women, ladies luncheon clubs, the New Labour party, Zonta, even Rotary. I found an amazing amount of agreement with what I was saying. Women across the country seemed to be disillusioned by the lack of integrity of the political process. They were sick of not being listened to. Time and again I was told that there had to be change—of both the government and the conduct of politics.

Back in 1984 many women had pinned their hopes on the Royal Commission on Social Policy. It had been a major plank in the Labour party's election platform, supported by the Minister of Women's Affairs, Ann Hercus, and the Prime Minister, David Lange. High profile social activists Ros Noonan and Anne Ballin had sat on the Commission. It had seemed like an opportunity to moderate the destructive social vision of the marketeers. I worked with Jo Lynch and others from the Women's Studies Association on a submission which spelled out the social destructiveness of competitive individualism. But when the Commission's report came out it was a letter to Santa rather than a plan of resistance. It did not provide a coherent alternative to the language of public choice theory, which insists that public policy be assessed on business criteria of short-term profit or loss. Parliament moved swiftly to discredit it. Ministers openly joked about using the report as a doorstop.

During the 1984 election Richard Prebble, then an opposition member of parliament, had barnstormed the country on the 'Save Rail' campaign. After the Labour party came to power it became quickly apparent that what this meant was not the retention of the only established, environmentally friendly, energy efficient, economic transportation system in New Zealand, but quite the opposite: liberated trucks thundering down our road system which was inadequate for the new traffic and in some cases began disintegrating.

By 1988 the sale of public assets seemed to have gained an unstoppable momentum. Deals were being made so fast the media barely had time to cover one before racing to the next. Richard Prebble, by now the Minister of State-owned Enterprises, appeared like a deranged Roman emperor whipping the troops on to certain defeat. With the restructuring of the Post Office, New Zealanders experienced directly the effects of policies based on denying the existence of a common good. Post offices had been a focal point in many communities, connecting individuals and providing a link in vital social services, whether with regional government agencies, such as the Department of Social Welfare, or the Ministry of Transport. Women—the majority of home workers—and the elderly, were most affected; they tended to be dependent on their immediate neighbourhood. The closure in February 1988 of over 430 post offices, many in small, isolated rural communities, exposed the real meaning of economic rationalism. 'Efficiency' meant travelling long distances and waiting in interminable queues to buy a stamp or collect Guaranteed Retirement Income.

We were all asking where the opposition to the new right was to come from. The Labour party had opened the door to this disastrous philosophy—a fact particularly painful to feminists, many of whom had held great hopes for Labour in 1984. Large numbers of women had worked for a Labour victory, and for the first time it had been secured by a majority of women's votes. In 1984, too, the largest group of women ever had entered parliament. Ominously Prime Minister David Lange had not appointed more than a token two to Cabinet. The unions were not providing much in the way of opposition to the new right. The reawakening of feminism in the seventies had seen a significant influx of women as union officials but not as leaders. I encountered Council of Trade Unions' president Ken Douglas twice in 1988 and was bewildered by his version of realpolitik. His attitude seemed to be that if the unions played along they would be seen as 'responsible', and the government would continue to consult with them. Even if such consultation was entirely farcical, it would, he insisted, be better than the deregulation of unions and the labour market, as threatened by the National party should it win in 1990. In the event, commitment to this corporatist vision hamstrung the unions' ability to defend themselves.

The 1990 election, as it happened, did not give women, unions, or anyone else a real choice in economic direction. By that time the only difference between the parties was how far along the spectrum of monetarism they were: they differed only on the extent of the roll-back of the welfare state, deregulation of the labour market, and Maori rights. It was not until 1992—when National finally agreed to do what Labour had managed to avoid, hold a referendum on electoral reform—that the public got a chance to express its feelings of helplessness and alienation. Unable to vote against the policies, it voted against the system that had allowed those policies to run rampant. Eighty-eight percent of those who voted supported a change to proportional representation, but politicians dismissed the results with the same contempt they had displayed towards the voice of the public for the last decade. Prime Minister Jim Bolger claimed that because only a million people had voted, it didn't count. It took a letter-writer to *The Evening Post* to point out that this was considerably more than had ever voted in a National or a Labour government.

The new right movement was arguably more successful in New Zealand than in any other western country. Here its proponents took over both of the major political parties. Their tactics became rapidly familiar. Exponents of the new right philosophy rarely entered public debate directly, but made skilful use of public relations. The agenda was presented not as political theory but as expert advice, the only rational, objective answer. They seized the economic high ground, using existing thinktanks and establishing their own when the need arose. The Centre for Independent Studies, despite its name, was dependent on the corporations which funded it. Exponents of the new right percolated their ideas through government policy advisory bodies and set up powerful lobby groups such as the Business Roundtable. Members of the Roundtable or their corporate interests soon dominated both parties and the machinery of government administration. 'There is no alternative'—TINA—became the comforting catch cry of successive governments, while beneficiaries marched, Maori went to court and feminists wrote articles attempting to expose the destructive assumptions on which the theories were based.

How had it happened? How had a small group of public service and academic economists, backed by an equally small group of businesspeople, taken over government policy-making virtually overnight? In 1984 a broad and unlikely coalition had voted the Labour party into power with one common purpose: to remove National Prime Minister Robert Muldoon. The new right wanted to get rid of Muldoon because he supported economic intervention and the welfare state, both anathema to their creed. People in the middle ground of politics had finally got fed up with his bellicose style degrading the political process. And the left were keen to get rid of his social conservatism, which manifested itself in things like an implacable opposition to abortion, adult adoption information or any alternative to the traditional male dominated/father absent kiwi family.

In the late seventies Muldoon had set out to destroy the traditional consensus around the welfare state in New Zealand. Since the thirties the welfare state had underwritten family formation and support—it was a reward for conformity, an inducement to raise families, state support for the 'good family man'. Between 1972 and 1975, under the Kirk government, Labour had, however, extended the welfare state to other social groups by introducing such measures as the Domestic Purposes Benefit.

In 1975 Muldoon introduced a generous vote-winning super-annuation package: his own wartime generation had become in reality the greatest beneficiaries of the welfare state. But he made a distinction between these worthy people and those he designated bludgers. He did not want the welfare state to support anybody who was not a member of what he fondly called 'Rob's mob'. Maori, sole mothers, ohu dwellers need not apply. The state, Muldoon believed, should not legitimise alternatives to the standard issue kiwi lifestyle.

The Domestic Purposes Benefit allowed women to live (just) independently of the patriarchal family. It was seen by feminists as one of the most important advances for women this century. But Muldoon saw it as underwriting marginal people. His Minister of Social Welfare, Bert Walker, had gone so far as to order his departmental snoops to count toothbrushes and shoes under the bed in the homes of Domestic Purposes Benefit recipients. Walker gave the famous chocolate biscuit speech, claiming that one of his informants had seen a woman on the Domestic Purposes Benefit buying chocolate biscuits. Clearly she was not being punished with the life of sexual and appetite deprivation decreed appropriate for women who strayed. Later, when he bitterly opposed the Adult Adoption Information Bill in 1985, Muldoon would praise women who had given up their babies for adoption into nice conventional families. These women had played by the rules and deserved to be protected from their 'unfortunate little mistakes'—as, of course, did the babies' fathers, wherever they were. The welfare state was traditionally pro-natalist: contraception was charged for, but maternity care was free. Under Muldoon, New Zealand remained the land of the free positive pregnancy test. If the test was negative, you paid; if it was positive, you enjoyed the fruits of the Maternity Services Benefit.

To feminists, Muldoon personified the smug face of the patriarchy. His own philanderings, and the trip of at least one of his girlfriends to Australia at a time when abortion was unavailable in New Zealand, seemed to epitomise the hypocrisy of the man and the power he wielded. Feminists saw him as using the state to enforce the double standard.

In 1984 the only thing the strange bedfellows opposing Muldoon had in common, apart from a desire to get rid of the

Prime Minister, was a sixties belief in personal freedom. The old left and new right were bound together only by this tenuous thread. Through their common purpose the Lange government came in with an almost unprecedented mandate for change. The question was, whose change? And for whom?

One of the most curious things about the Lange landslide was that the Labour party came into power without any substantial economic policy. What policy there was consisted of vague generalisations designed to be all things to all people. What most of the electorate—and probably David Lange himself—did not know was that advocates of drastic free market-style changes had installed themselves in key positions in government departments, particularly Treasury. It would later become apparent that they had a strategy to influence the administration of the state through a programme of state service reform. They were able to make strategic placements of adherents of the new right philosophy; these people in turn were able to vet appointees to significant policy posts. Far from just influencing party policies, the new right had worked their way into the fabric of the public service—or what remained of it after restructuring turned vast slews into that strange hybrid, the state-owned enterprise.

The electorate was confused about the fact that these changes were being instituted under a Labour government. Many women smelt a rat but few were confident enough to take on the language of econo-drivel. Most of us have tended to see economics as brrm-brrm-twin-carbs stuff, what the boys talked about when conversation about their four wheeled penises wound down. Chatter about *the* economy seemed to sum up the male approach to politics, quantification being just another cop-out from the personal.

The only explicit economic theory available within the women's movement had been a socialist one. The old left, however, had minimised issues of gender and race by reducing them to class. The Trotskyists had a well developed analysis which focused on capitalism's need for the family, and they consequently campaigned on issues of reproductive rights. These positions were significant in winning reproductive freedoms. But most of the middle class women's movement was not connected with these left wing groups. The only other available view was that of the separatist, alternative lifestyle movement, which recommended draining energy from the system by dropping out of the economy completely. Most women rejected this, fearing it would drain energy from them, not the system. The majority took the economic underpinnings of the country for granted. Like most New Zealanders, they believed that a moderate prosperity was intrinsic to New Zealand, just part of the way things were.

Without an institutional base, the opposition to the Roger Douglas juggernaut was a ragtag of marginal groups. The most effectively organised resistance came from Maori, whose values are unequivocally opposed to competitive individualism. Legal action based on the Treaty of Waitangi brought Maori interests immediately into head-on conflict with the misappropriation and sale of public assets. Maori were able to slow down the process and protect all New Zealanders from the full force of the multinationals' new land-grabbing, asset-stripping imperialism. Maori are, however, now being punished for their skilful use of the legal system. The scapegoating of Maori people as one of the chief causes of our economic woes has given a dangerous boost to racism in the country.

It took women longer to latch on to what was happening, not least because the Lange government had come to power in 1984 with an extensive and detailed women's policy, the first in New Zealand's history. The policy supported the establishment of a Ministry of Women's Affairs, dramatic increases in child care funding, equal pay for work of equal value, and a raft of other traditional feminist demands such as more representation for women on government bodies. What the policy did not address— and what would be in retrospect the one thing which let the fast moving Douglas economic 'reforms' occur in those early months with little effective and united protest from feminists—was economic policy. Had women been privy to the confidential papers which floated around Treasury, and between that department and the Minister of Finance, they might have been alerted to the fact that the engineers of the level playing field planned to send women to the penalty box.

At heart, although the new right claimed to have progressive and radical new solutions, their philosophic underpinning was destined to carry us back to the social atrocities of the nineteenth century. They planned to sweep away all the hard won gains of 150 years of organising by women, workers and colonised peoples. 'It got to the stage,' one feminist recalled, 'that if I had read in *The Dominion* one day that the Business Roundtable proposed taking away the vote from women I would not have been at all surprised. It would be relatively easy to make a case that since only market leaders deserved a say in running the country, having women voting was inefficient.'

Feminists had worked hard to persuade the Labour party that if women were to overcome historical inequalities, we would need some assistance. We demanded, for example, employment equity legislation to overcome the undervaluing of women's work, and to incorporate unpaid work into the economic equation. We sought greater government funding of child care to enable women to have more work opportunities. The new right operated from a narrow ideological base. If someone wanted something, the theory went, they would be prepared to pay for it. If, for example, child care was highly desired, people would be prepared to fork out, and child care workers would be paid more. Although the theory was transparently flawed—in this case the people most in need of child care were the people least able to pay very much for it—it was repeated endlessly like a mantra. But behind the chanting were women whose situations were getting worse.

The 1987 share market crash ought to have signalled to New Zealand that there were dangers in being locked into the global economy and in wholesale deregulation. Instead it had the opposite effect, creating a climate of insecurity in which New Zealanders were ready to listen to ever more radical and desperate solutions. Indeed we were desperate to believe that someone had a solution. Even so, few realised that the National government elected in 1990 planned to carry national asset stripping to new heights with an even more extreme programme of privatisation and labour market deregulation.

What was wrong with the economy, we were told, was that the poor were paid too much for doing too little and the rich were paid too little for doing too much. The answer was said to be to create incentives. This entailed increasing the gap between the downtrodden, who needed the lash of fear to make them work harder, and those whom American feminist and social commentator Barbara Ehrenreich had christened the uptrodden —the entrepreneurs, big corporations who needed juicier plums if they were to hang around long enough for their firms to pay taxes.

By 1992 National Prime Minister Jim Bolger was openly exhorting the country to worship the rich as heroes. Like the new right, he failed to mention that his newfound heroes, far from trickling their wealth on to New Zealand's needy, were actually consolidating it around the shores of Sydney harbour. Nor did he point out that New Zealand manufacturers had been closing down their factories in New Zealand so they could open them in Fiji, where Indian women would be paid seven dollars a day for doing the work New Zealand women had done for seven dollars an hour. In six years 120,000 jobs have been lost, including 82,000 in manufacturing, a sector in which many women are (or at least were) employed.

Women suffered enormously from the deregulation of the labour market. When this was pushed to the extreme with the Employment Contracts Act 1991, the first unions to fall over were those such as the Clerical Workers' Union which represented low paid, women-dominated occupations. To survive, others joined sector unions. Small groups of secretaries and canteen workers, for example, joined the Engineers' Union hoping that the industrial muscle of the male workers would protect rather than swamp them.

After the 1988 Women's Studies Association conference, a number of women and I had formed a group called The Women's Agenda to push political parties to design policies with women in mind. Since women voters outnumbered men, we printed bumper stickers proclaiming '1990 is coming: women will elect the next government'—a bitter irony, as it turned out, since the National government which got in was even more contemptuous of women's push for equality than the Labour government had been. Indeed, its first legislative act was to repeal the new Employment Equity Act which was to ensure equal pay for work of equal value.

In 1992 we used the money that had been generated by selling the bumper stickers to print new ones supporting a change to the Mixed Member Proportional (MMP) system in the referendum on electoral reform. It was an indication of how far the power of the new right had eroded by then that our money was not wasted. The vote for a change to proportional representation was huge, despite—or perhaps because of—such a change being bitterly and publicly opposed by the Business Roundtable, the Employers' Federation and most members of parliament and officials of both parties, including the woman to have reached the highest political rank, former Labour Deputy Prime Minister Helen Clark.

In its campaign to thwart electoral reform, the Business Roundtable went to the lengths of commissioning thinktank-for-hire, CS First Boston, to write a report. In an earlier report, *The Inequity of Pay Equity*, CS First Boston's Penelope Brook argued that pay equity patronised women's abilities. She and two male co-authors dutifully produced a report for the Business Roundtable which pronounced that a vote for proportional representation would deliver the death blow to the great economic miracle we were now (even if we were too silly to see it) experiencing. In the event, the public's perverse lack of rationality would be exceeded only by the size of its vote for change.

To have women such as Brook fronting and defending policies which many feminists—and by this time women throughout the country—considered destructive has presented feminists like myself with a dilemma. How do we oppose policies on the grounds they are unfair to women when women present and defend them—women, furthermore, whose success is interpreted as being what some feminists seek for us all? Another aspect caused considerable soul searching. After the seventies stress on co-operation, consciousness raising and shared experience, the feminist movement in the eighties had focused on getting women into positions of power and decision-making, in the expectation that once they were there they would promote policies in the interests of women. But by the beginning of the nineties a number of high profile women, including some 'former' feminists, were closely identified with market policies. In a number of cases, they were public apologists for them.

The Minister of Finance was a woman. The Minister of Social Welfare was a woman. Women such as Judith Aitken, a convener of the 1972 United Women's Convention, former nursing head Margaret Bazley, veteran feminist Maris O'Rourke, and Marijke

Robinson, a founder member of Women's Electoral Lobby, were heading government departments or were in their senior management teams. Claudia Scott, a leading exponent of public choice theory, the new right gospel, was head of the Master in Public Policy diploma course at Victoria University. In this position, she could have a major impact on the production and placement in the public service of fluent speakers of the bizarre language which *The Evening Post* columnist Mary Varnham has described as 'jerkish'.

I found the messages emanating from these women disturbing. Judith Aitken (who was to become head of the Ministry of Women's Affairs) was corporate relations manager of Electricorp in 1985, under leading new righter Rod Deane. When Electricorp announced the 'shedding' of at least 828 workers, it was Aitken who broke the news, proclaiming the corporation's right wing philosophy in *The Evening Post* of 12 September 1987, 'We are not a supply-driven organisation any more. We are now driven by the market.' She explained further that government departments such as Health and Social Welfare had been advised to prepare for extra demand on their services.

In 1988 Aitken was shoulder tapped to head the Ministry of Women's Affairs. Many feminists saw her appointment as an attempt to dampen down feminist opposition to current economic policies. Former head Mary O'Regan, in the period before her resignation in 1988, had signalled that the Ministry of Women's Affairs was developing feminist critiques of economic policy and had negotiated to hire Victoria University economist Pru Hyman, who pursued a feminist economic analysis, on a year's contract.

In the late eighties I wanted to hear the Ministry comment publicly on the disastrous impact the government's economic policies were having on women. But with Aitken at the helm it did not comment, and had in fact dramatically wound down its communication with women in the community. The Ministry became a model of the new right's detached ministry whose sole accountability was to its minister. For the theorists, the role of the public service is not to provide the public with a service but to defend the purity of the 'free' economy against a predatory populace and their vote-hungry politicians. Only speakers of jerkish are considered objective: they have not been captured by 'interest groups' such as women.

As chair of the Second Sweating Commission in 1990 I toured the country and heard 300 submissions from retail workers about conditions in our lowest paid industry. I was amazed by how clearly ordinary women, from supermarket checkout operators and shelf fillers to apprentice butchers, saw the flaws of the prevailing economic policies. With a perspicacity which appeared to have eluded high ranking government ministers, not to mention well paid and perked Treasury officials, these women understood precisely the connections between the flogging off of New Zealand, the running down of local industry with its large scale layoffs, and the deregulation of the labour market.

Chatter about market upturns, economic u-turns and deficit downturns couldn't disguise the fact that the aim of the exercise had been to provide the cheapest possible labour in the worst possible conditions—not, as we'd been told, to lead us towards a high wage economy. Sixteen-year-old full-time workers were earning a gross income of $7,690 a year. It was clear to those at the checkout counter that this could never be the basis for economic recovery.

Two years later, in February 1992, I again toured the country, this time as a member of the People's Select Committee. In the 1991 budget the Bolger National government had introduced an extreme new right package. Benefits were slashed, unions were reduced to the legal status of the local bowling club, and people who left their jobs were to be subjected to a terrifying six months in which they were eligible for a benefit of $68 a week on condition that once they got the dole they paid back this pittance. By this time, according to evidence presented to the Select Committee, one in three young people leaving school was going on to the unemployment benefit. Those 20- to 24-year-olds who found a job earned a median full-time annual income of $20,241 if they were male and $19,942 if they were female. For women this represented a meagre $2,100 improvement in 20 years. The fruits of feminists' struggles had been waylaid by the economic miracle. The Select Committee came face to face with the reality of hunger, the desolation of homelessness and the isolation of poverty. We met a disintegrating society in person—the low paid and beneficiaries alike, who had been shoved into the new card-carrying underclass.

Overwhelmingly, the people who came forward to give evidence were women. Many were equipped with detailed budgets. These showed no money for household maintenance or insurance, and almost none for personal care. Single people often had about $30 to $35 a week for food, clothing and transport. Whole families had about $50 to $60. The idea of having $100 a week to feed a family of four was unimaginable luxury. Deprivation is cumulative. I remember a woman whose husband had left her with four children. She had struggled to raise them and keep them motivated at school despite their perpetual hunger. Now, thanks to the iniquitous 'user pays', she faced years of trying to support them through tertiary education. When they had finished she would be in her fifties, the least employable age. How then could she save to support herself in her old age? A woman who heard this commented that when she was on the Domestic Purposes Benefit herself in the seventies, she had the real possibility of an end in sight, but for all their efforts these people could never improve their situation.

If the aim of the policies had been—as Roger Douglas and his successor, National party Finance Minister Ruth Richardson, claimed—to unleash entrepreneurial vigour, it had done so only among a small elite. For the rest it had created a permanently demoralised majority whose only hope of acting as rational utility maximisers lay, like some of the entrepreneurs of the 1987 market crash, in engaging in criminal activity.

New Zealanders had been subjected to an unfortunate economic experiment that few politicians other than David Lange (after 1987), former National MP Winston Peters and Alliance leader Jim Anderton had dared suggest was anything other than a panacea. For all the ministrations of Logos public pelations and Saatchi and Saatchi advertising, the patient had remained obstinately unconvinced. By 1992 the chief achievement of the economic miracle was a record level of public cynicism and disillusionment with politicians and the political process. Not surprisingly—as according to official statistics nearly 15 percent of the total workforce and 25 percent of the Maori workforce and the Pacific Islands workforce were now jobless.

Politicians of both parties have been engaged in a flight from reality. In the *Auckland Star* of 25 October 1992 Bolger insisted we were engaged in a 'high wire act', edging from the old to the new economy. Identifying a national fear of flying as the key problem he, like the Labour government before him, exhorted his own nerve in the fearless pursuit of unpopular policies. Anyone who shook the wire by questioning policy was, the Prime Minister advised, placing the whole country in danger.

As if to demonstrate the ubiquity of the zipperless policy package, the same page of the *Auckland Star* reported that Peter Dunne, Labour MP for Ohariu, had urged Australian Labour MPs to adopt the policies so fearlessly pursued in New Zealand. Dunne cheerfully assured those alarmed about the downside of such policies that high unemployment and low economic growth were 'non-issues' in New Zealand. In a dazzling impersonation of Rowan Atkinson's Mr Bean, he seemed blind to the irony of urging his Australian counterparts to adopt policies which had almost destroyed his own party.

In 1992 popular resistance to new right policies found several focuses, in particular a successful campaign against the sale of the Ports of Auckland, and growing support for the Alliance, which called for an end to free market policies and a halt to asset sales. By the end of the year, after a success in the Auckland local body elections, the Alliance was registering 33 percent electoral support in national opinion polls.

But while the public was heading in one direction, the State Services Commission was heading in the other. A 1991 study had looked at whether the $380 million by then spent annually on contracting policy analysis represented value for money. The Commission's subsequent report revealed an extraordinarily narrow conception of what was relevant to policy analysis. Typically, those with any knowledge of a particular social area were suspected of 'capture' or 'advocacy'. Ignorance was the only surefire way to avoid bias. Rational Man, knowing nothing and being influenced by nobody who does, would be a suitable recruit. The Master in Public Policy diploma course at Victoria University was specifically recommended as a preferred training route.

In the eighties and nineties New Zealand feminists were

catapulted not on to a level playing field (the jerkish term we'd come to dread) but on to one which tilted ever more precariously. The edicts of the new right and the cult of individualism ran counter to just about every value we had. From being social reformers we had to become economists, able to bat back the whacky arguments of Treasury, the Business Roundtable and brainwashed or weak politicians.

Many women looked for some kind of leadership to Women's Studies programmes, which by the late eighties existed in all but one New Zealand university (Lincoln). Some of the most cogent analyses of new right policies and fallacies have come from these departments, or from feminist academics in other departments. But recognition that policy advice was one of New Zealand's few growth industries posed some difficult dilemmas. One option was to position Women's Studies so that it could draw closer to the makers of the new order. The Women's Studies department at Waikato University chose this route. Its foundation professor sought to establish the department as the provider of a particular form of policy expertise. The department's professional identity was seen as producing recruits for upper levels of government administration, and a male teacher was hired from Victoria University's Master of Public Policy programme. This stance locates local and community issues on the periphery. The Women's Studies department at Waikato University has withdrawn from distance education, and minimised community interaction. In their view, strength is not to be found in the grass roots but in securing a transcendent analytical vantage point. The claim to centrality positions Women's Studies as a route to high achievement for women. To locate Women's Studies at the opposite pole—resisting rather than acquiescing in the current restructuring of the world—is to choose a less powerful and rewarded position and to be exposed to personal risk. Articulating an alternative future takes energy and is slow, requiring the patient building of alliances, the careful nurturing of community links.

After a decade of galloping monetarism, the truth has now dawned on all but a few grey-suited market men in a cluster of buildings around The Terrace: the theory doesn't work. A dramatic realignment is going on in the New Zealand public's political allegiance. The emergence of the Alliance has slowed the momentum of new right certainty, presenting the electorate with more than a choice of *Rogernomes II* and *Return of the Rogernomes*. It has already moved political debate back towards the centre. In the Wellington Central parliamentary by-election in 1992 the existence of a viable Alliance candidate in the political heartland pushed the Labour party into a rapid distancing from its recent past.

In 1992 I chose to join the Green party and support the Alliance in Wellington Central. I was attracted to the Green party because of its policy of gender equity in all positions and its realisation that the sustainability of the physical and social environment is the basis of any economic policy that makes long-term sense. The Alliance begins to draw together the New Labour party's awareness of how policy creates poverty, and its long experience with the defence of working conditions, Mana Motuhake's understanding that the Treaty of Waitangi is integral to the development of a peaceable society, and the Green party's insistence on moving from short-term measures of profit to long-term social, economic, personal and environmental goals. I have found that working with the Green party's co-deputy leaders Sandra Lee of Mana Motuhake and Jeanette Fitzsimmons of the Green party has reawakened my hope. Both have courage, staying power and long herstories of political integrity. Both look forward to a possible, liveable future.

I am now the Alliance candidate for Wellington's Onslow electorate in the 1993 parliamentary elections, standing against Peter Dunne of the Labour party's right wing. As one of 12 Alliance spokespeople I have responsibility for health, women, and children and young people, and have a seat ex-officio on the Alliance Council. Participation in political organisation at the national level has proved extraordinarily interesting. In contrast to the fragmented, divided organisation depicted in the media, I have found the Alliance to be strong and intact. It has successfully substituted the false unity of the party whip with respect for diversity, and a commitment to work together for a common cause. We have worked co-operatively to develop policy which restores integrity to the political system by presenting voters with clear options.

Who'll Marry Her Now?

MARY VARNHAM

PICTURE YOURSELF in the early sixties: a flappy teenager with kiss-curls, gathered cotton skirt cinched with a wide elastic belt, oyster pink nail polish and a stack of Beatles records. Look at me, I'm Sandra Dee. A *good* girl, too scared not to be. You slept with Paul's photo under your pillow, but when it came to the real thing, flesh and blood specimens of the male species, *boys*, who knew what could happen? Who even knew how it happened?

Consider yourself warned. Well, in so many words. Your mother ummed, aahed. 'Oh yes, I know all about that, mum'—to put her out of her misery. But you were never quite sure. All you knew was that boys were dangerous, predatory. But they could be tamed. That was your job—to stop them *going too far*, and turn them into husbands who mowed lawns, earned money, fathered children (how, you'd find out soon enough) and went to the footie on Saturday afternoons. And when it came to getting married, men did not want damaged goods.

> Sex was something you didn't do. In holidays from boarding school I would hear about girls who had disgraced their families and had shotgun weddings and how terrible it was. But I had a strong sex drive so I used to neck with boys at parties and get

covered in love bites. I wouldn't do 'it' though. I didn't know the facts of life. I'd had one biology lesson at school which showed the foetus already in the womb. I had no idea how it got there. I'd never seen an erect penis. I believed you got pregnant instantly you did 'it', but I wasn't sure what 'it' was.[1]

Whatever else, IT was part of your future.

I remember boys taking me home from school dances and doing the dry grind and I would think, 'This is sex, I'm meant to be enjoying it.' I found it sort of scary. I thought, 'This must be what women have to put up with. This must be what having a boyfriend is all about.'

Boys fumbled with the clasp of your bra, put their hands down your pants, stuck their tongues in your mouth. Stopping them doing any more than this was your responsibility. If you failed you might get into trouble and it would be your fault not his, because boys, well, they couldn't help themselves. If you were lucky, the boy would marry you, *you*, in a white dress— with a pink petticoat, just so you wouldn't exactly be lying to god or the neighbours about being a virgin at the altar.

If you weren't lucky and your parents wouldn't let you marry him, because he was a Catholic or a Maori or just not our sort of people, or (total humiliation) he would not marry you, you would have to go away and have the baby somewhere else, have it adopted out. No one would ever know, a secret, in the family. Don't let it *ruin your life*.

I was unbelievably naive. I hardly even knew how you got pregnant. Close friends would suddenly leave town for nine months and it didn't occur to me that they hadn't just decided Wanganui or New Plymouth were fun places to live. With one very close friend I didn't find out the truth until 10 years later when she was having severe emotional problems because of what had happened.

But in practical terms you didn't know how to avoid getting into trouble, other than by saying no. In the middle of it. No. No-o-o. No!!! Even though, if you forgot the fear and the voices for a minute, you could feel your blood racing. A thought: Maybe I am a bad girl.

---

1 This essay is based on research and interviews with twelve women born in the forties and fifties.

And there were boys who obviously hadn't had the lecture, because when you said no they didn't take much notice. You hoped, prayed, that there was quite a lot further to go before you got anywhere near Too Far. Fear and loathing and strange sensations in the back of someone's father's Ford Zephyr. 'I hardly even knew how you got pregnant. My idea of contraception was the man saying, "Don't worry, everything will be fine."' 'Withdrawal was the only method of contraception I knew. After I'd done the full act three times with my boyfriend I got pregnant.'

Suddenly they were men, not boys.

> I spent the second half of the sixties at university in Dunedin. The first year I cuddled and kissed and when things got hot I pretended I had a period. I was still a virgin. In my second year I had a boyfriend who wanted to go *the whole way* and I thought I'd better oblige, otherwise he might go off with someone else.
>
> Being a good Presbyterian girl, I decided to be sensible and get myself on the pill. You couldn't get it from Student Health. The university was opposed to male and female students living together, let alone having sex. In 1967 they suspended a male student who was flatting platonically with two women. James K Baxter wrote a poem about it, 'An Ode to Mixed Flatting'—'Many's the time I've dipped my wick in Castle Street'. I remember it vividly because I was living in Castle Street at the time and I thought, 'God, I hope my mother doesn't read it.'

You and your boyfriend (lucky enough to have one) bopped to the Rolling Stones: 'I can't get no satisfaction.' Wow, rock'n'roll. Born to be wild, baby won't you light my fire? Good vibrations. And then? 'Oh, sex before marriage was extremely furtive. You didn't usually have anywhere to do it so you made do with the back of the car, or a room at a party where someone might appear at any moment.' Some people did it fully dressed. 'He would jiggle on top of me and then, boom, it would be over. I used to lie awake at night worrying about whether sperm could travel through clothes.'

You did it, but didn't talk about it. Woman as island.

> My first sexual encounters weren't very satisfactory. I didn't know what I was supposed to experience during sex, other than some hazy notion of true love and a warm glow afterwards. I hardly knew what an orgasm was. I remember having orgasmic feelings and being a bit embarrassed.

Notes were not compared. Men were protected.

I became sexually active in 1965 and didn't have an orgasm until 1975. My lovers were inept. They wouldn't have known what a female orgasm was, didn't have a clue. Probably still don't. No one I associated with discussed sexual habits or feelings. I had no idea this wasn't all there was to it.

Men were protected.

My first sexual experience was rape. I was sent to report on a Yugoslav trade mission that was in town and I got talking to a local Yugoslav man. Under some pretence, he took me to a secluded bay and raped me. It was incredibly painful. I was 19. I remember going into the bathroom in my flat and looking in the mirror and thinking, 'Well, at least I've had sex.'

You were always trying to get the pill. Prescriptions were for six months, sometimes only three. Back to the doctor, but who, this time? What story this time?

My friends and I used to borrow each other's pills. I got pregnant when I was 23. You could not get an abortion in New Zealand so I went off to Sydney. I arrived with a list of doctors and I can remember standing in a phone booth ringing them up. The abortion itself was the most frightening experience I had ever had. The doctor said, 'If you don't stop shrieking I'll throw you into the street.' I remember later standing in a post office sending postcards to my friends in New Zealand with blood dripping on to the floor.

This was the sexual revolution. We were supposed to be doing it everywhere, letting it all hang out, repressing nothing. Sex was going to make us free. Sex was going to make us popular. Inhibitions were embarrassing.

It was a male fantasy run wild, everything men had always wanted. All these women available for sex and we were brainwashed into thinking we were supposed to want to have sex all the time, with no real intimacy.

There is now a vivid, unrehearsed consensus.

The sexual revolution was great for men. I remember men slobbering over me and I just went along with it. Our mothers were probably more realistic about sex—they realised it had its limitations. Whereas we thought, especially in those early days, that sex would give us everything—love, happiness, intimacy. Of course it didn't and we've never quite recovered.

When the sexual revolution happened I went out with heaps of men and never used contraception. I'd been brought up a Catholic and I thought contraception was wrong. You were supposed to do it for love. I spent every month going through this extraordinary worry about whether I was pregnant.

In 1971 early women's liberationist Sue Kedgley told a hallful of Rotary club members, 'It's not your penises we've been envying all these centuries—it's your freedom.' She had bought Robin Morgan's book *Sisterhood is Powerful* in Australia, and New Zealand Customs had tried to confiscate it for indecency. Words like penis, vagina and orgasm were indecent. Decent people didn't talk like that. Decent *women* especially didn't talk like that.

What did decent women do? 'The message from my parents was, be sexy but don't give in. You must be attractive—there's nothing worse than a butch woman. But never enjoy sex. It was very confusing.' The mini was de rigeur. You tottered down The Terrace in chunky tweed suits with skirts so short that bending over a filing cabinet required a unique feat of muscular control. Dedicated followers of fashion. In those days fashions were much more universal. If minis were in you couldn't buy anything else, wouldn't *wear* anything else.

Legs became the ultimate female body part for the sexual revolution. In train of minis came hot pants with long skirts on top, buttons open to the waist.

That said it all. You were sexually available, sending out mating signals in all directions, but you could still button up and look like a suburban housewife at a Plunket meeting if you had to. We were expected to grow up as good, normal, healthy, sexually dysfunctional New Zealand women.

American novelist and poet Erica Jong coined the most memorable phrase of the sexual revolution, the zipless fuck. Sex without impediment. Sex without hang-ups. Sex for its own sake.

The idea was that you would go out and sleep with somebody and then you'd develop the relationship. But my choice in men was terrible. They had no idea what they were doing sexually, nor did they have the interest or commitment to spend time getting it right. I put a lot of time and energy into unsatisfactory relationships.

If I had sex with someone I would develop a whole elaborate scenario about our future life together and the men would rarely measure up. A lot of women in our generation did that. They grew up mistaking sex for love and hoping that a sexual experience would lead to love. We were fed a lot of romantic images in books and on television that reinforced this. And the myth suited men because it meant we were dead keen to fall into bed with them.

In 1989 Lillian Rubin would sum up the era in *Ms* magazine:

While the sexual revolution of the sixties freed women to say yes, it also too often disabled them from saying no. For some time, therefore, sexual freedom lived side by side with sexual exploitation.

One of the women Rubin interviewed said:

God, when I think how naive we were. 'There was a hell of a lot of abuse and manipulation in those relationships, a hell of a lot, and a lot of women look back and see how they were used in the name of sexual freedom ... women [now] feel much more able to make choices about whom they'll sleep with, or even whether they'll be sexual at all.

When the new wave of feminism began to filter belatedly into New Zealand in the early seventies, there was an unconscious assumption that it would address the conflict and tension that had arisen around sex.

A whole generation of women had experienced the most painful conflict. In the sixties you were made to feel that if you didn't consent to sex virtually on demand you had no future as a woman. But at the same time we wanted what women have always wanted—caring, supportive relationships. Most of the time we didn't get them.

In retrospect, it wasn't all the men's fault.

We weren't looking in places where caring, sensual, nice men were. Men who had values were uncool. We tended not to know the sort who didn't want to have sex with a woman as soon as he met her. We thought men like that were wet and uninteresting.

Some of the early women's liberationists had pointed out that women lived on more intimate terms with their oppressors than any other oppressed group in history. Behind the bedroom door, power was almost absolute. Most husbands assumed it was their right, even their duty, to 'take' their wives sexually whenever they felt like it. It was their wives' duty to submit right back.

In the sixties this 'right' had expanded exponentially. All men, married or not, got to feel they had the right to women's bodies. All women were required to be sexually available. And the fact was that for most their primary sexual orientation was towards men.

So the question arose: Could you be a feminist, battling against the male establishment, and still sleep with men? Could you share your homes, lives and bodies with your oppressors, and not betray the sisterhood? Even Germaine Greer, usually intellectually fearless, seemed reluctant to tackle this ideological paradox. In *The Female Eunuch* she focused on making women less sexually passive. Equality consisted in getting *your* rocks off. 'Love-making,' Greer complained, 'has become another male skill. . . . The skills that the Wife of Bath used to make her husbands swink, the athletic sphincters of the Tahitian girls who can keep their men inside them all night, are still unknown to us.'

Masters and Johnson had published *Human Sexual Response* a few years earlier. It had been the perfect handbook for the sexual revolution. Through clinically observing men and women having sexual intercourse or masturbating, American science had been able to reduce sex to a simple matter of pressing the right buttons to get the right responses. It was all a bit like making the perfect omelette. Greer objected to 'the veritable clitoromania' which had resulted.

> The banishment of the fantasy of the vaginal orgasm is ultimately a service, but the substitution of the clitoral orgasm for genuine gratification may turn out to be a disaster for sexuality. . . . The process described by the experts, in which the man dutifully does the rounds of the erogenous zones, spends an equal amount of time on each nipple, turns his attention to the clitoris (usually too directly), leads through the stages of digital or lingual stimulation and then politely lets himself into the vagina . . . is laborious and inhumanly computerised.

Real gratification, Greer pointed out, was not enshrined in a tiny cluster of nerves but in the sexual involvement of the whole person. If we localised female response in the clitoris we imposed on women 'the same limitation of sex which had stunted the male's response'. Ouch, performance anxiety! We should hold out 'not just for orgasm but for ecstasy'.

Ecstasy. *Ecstasy?*

> I didn't have decent sex until I went overseas when I was 24. New Zealand men were hopeless. They thought the whole idea was to get their rocks off and you might feel something along the way. They didn't know what—and the trouble was neither did we. I spent a lot of time wondering what all the fuss was about. Later, it was a revelation to go out with a man in London who knew what a female erogenous zone was.

And some of us were still holding out, period. Who knew why? Well of course you did. You didn't want to be bad, a slut, a tart, a bike, easy, loose. But if you didn't give in you were something even worse—a tease. It was all so complicated.

> Even though Student Health was dishing out the pill by the late sixties, I spent my varsity years doing everything but fucking. I had a boyfriend and when I was with him I'd feel something moving in me but I was determined not to Have Sex. Casual or recreational sex wasn't a concept for me. So I'd suck him off. He didn't know how to bring me to orgasm so I'd be incredibly frustrated. When I finally decided to lose my virginity, get it over and done with, I chose an old friend who was going overseas a few weeks afterwards. I figured he could be faithful to me that long. He turned out to have a two inch cock and to be a lousy lover.
>
> Later I went overseas myself. I was 25. I took a year's supply of the pill and tried to join the free love generation. I had three torrid affairs on the boat going to England but free love didn't work for me. I found I couldn't just fuck and leave, and I got quite emotionally screwed up. Deep down, I didn't want to be promiscuous because of the bad girl image of my childhood.

In 1973 Sue Kedgley, still then one of the few New Zealand feminists to have tackled the subject of sex openly, told the BBC's Alan Whicker that the New Zealand male's idea of sex was a thrusting penis: he wouldn't know a clitoris if he came across one. The programme sent shockwaves through suburban living rooms when it was shown on national television, making Kedgley relieved that she had already moved to New York and was not around 'to take the flak from what was just a simple factual remark'.

This was the rugby society. Men performed, scored, cut notches in belts and prided themselves on their lack of romantic skill. Such affectations were the realm of sissies, pansies, poofs, Frenchmen. And, in their fathers' day, American marines.

> When I was a kid my family would be walking down the street on Friday night and there'd be a couple strolling along holding hands, or with their arms around each other. My father would rail on about how disgusting it was, how we never used to have *that sort of thing* before the Yanks came. He saw open displays of affection as inalienable proof of the collapse of moral standards.

A hard fought for tradition of Victorian repression. The free love generation of the sixties watched the film of James Joyce's *Ulysses* in sexually segregated cinemas. Women: Monday, Wednesday and Friday; men: Tuesday, Thursday and Saturday.

Marriage was to unveil the mysteries. You would know and experience everything. But women in permanent relationships were not experiencing the expected nirvana.

> When I was married I used to feel you had to consent to sex—it was part of the deal. You could be tired or have a sore toe for two weeks but eventually you'd run out of excuses. You had to grin and bear it.
>
> Even when I became a feminist I didn't talk to anyone about sex. I went to consciousness raising but I don't remember talking about sex. We were obsessed with who did the dishes, discrimination at work, political theory, women's health and contraception—nice safe issues. I think we sensed that if we talked about sex it would open a minefield and we wouldn't know how to deal with it.

Feminist true confession:

> I was out there trying to change the world but in the bedroom I was completely non-assertive. My sexual relationship with my husband was terrible. I had a view of male sexuality based on Mick Jagger— you know, man as sexual aggressor. Women had to be attractive, desirable, relaxed and multi-orgasmic.
>
> I felt I didn't measure up and my husband reinforced that belief. During sex he showed no emotion or even recognition. There was never any foreplay, just a poke on the bum to see if I was awake. In

all our marriage he never spent more than 10 minutes making love
to me. It was as though he was hammering a nail into a board.

After we broke up I asked him what he thought was happening
for me during sex. He said he knew some women weren't able to
have orgasms and he assumed I was one of them. He didn't see
any need to examine himself.

Feminism didn't help.

It increased the pressure if anything. I remember trying to talk
about my sexual difficulties at a feminist meeting and the women
made me feel like a freak. I mean, men were hopeless so why
worry about what sort of sex you had with them?

Like Greer, those New Zealand feminists bold enough to talk
about sex not just as a minor sideline but as a major philosophic
issue, focused on mechanics. They read *The Myth of the Vaginal
Orgasm* and ran how-to sessions.

The movement was in the full pursuit of the clitoral orgasm. At a
United Women's Convention I went to a workshop on masturbation where women said how liberating it was and talked about
the use of fingers, dildos et cetera. They showed a film which didn't
match my experience at all. I went away feeling there was something wrong with me because I didn't enjoy masturbation and
needed a penis to come.

Feminist joke: What's the difference between a man and a
vibrator? Answer: A vibrator can't put out the garbage.

Whatever excuses you made for men, they were in the end
men, culturally oppressive and philosophically unacceptable. The
male establishment, male power structures, male culture—whatever you called it, you could not escape the fact it was made up of
men just like the one you had slept with the night before and
shared marmalade with over the breakfast table. If you were a
politically active heterosexual feminist you lived a life of curious
denial.

I was constantly attending women's meetings, fighting to get laws
changed—matrimonial property, equal pay, action against domestic
violence and sexual abuse. I would get thoroughly charged up and
then I'd go out with some guy and find myself reverting
to some dreadful sexual stereotype, waiting for him to call me,

dressing in a sexy way when I went out with him. And, of course, if he didn't want me sexually I would feel inadequate.

The tug of the old—it was not easy to relinquish your personal future.

> I separated sex from men's other behaviour. I might see their attitudes and behaviour in other areas as totally at odds with my feminism but I accepted their sexual behaviour. I chose not to see it as a problem. The conflict between my personal behaviour and the feminist principles I espoused was therefore dramatic. In my professional life I was capable of being very assertive but privately, if you want to keep a man in your life, you didn't express yourself freely.

When it came to applying the maxim that the personal was the political, sex turned out to be the cutting edge.

> I would sometimes sit up late reading these powerful books by overseas feminists like Susan Brownmiller's *Against Our Will* about rape and I'd be feeling pretty emotional, upset and angry at the way men treated women. Then I'd crawl into bed and my partner would start groping me, as though it was his *right* to do this. And if I complained he would act hurt or angry, as though there were something wrong with me.

Even men who supported feminist goals such as equal pay, affordable child care and shared parenting baulked when it came to the bedroom. Not only was sex their right as men, it was a biological necessity. What's more they knew that, however much women might resist, they loved sex. If the right buttons were tweaked à la Masters and Johnson, the normal healthy woman would go off like a rocket.

The male sense of entitlement, combined with the rugby changing room model of masculinity, had led to a devastating level of sexual ineptitude. Gordon McLauchlan in his 1976 book *The Passionless People* reported a doctor telling him

> Sex is the awkward unpleasant bit of the social life of a woman that she has to put up with as best she can. There are almost zero bits of affection and tenderness and warm, loving attention.

McLauchlan coined the term passionless poking. Close your eyes and think of Palmerston North.

By the eighties many women were no longer prepared to put up with this and started demanding better.

> Once women started comparing notes, feminism became the biggest kick in the balls imaginable for male sexuality. The fact emerged that there were a lot of hopeless lovers out there.

Some women had opted out long before, or never opted in. As feminism progressed, heterosexual women found it harder to ignore their own ideological inconsistency and lesbians were able to claim the moral high ground. 'We don't let anybody touch our brains/ We will never ever plug into the mains/ We are overtaking on a single lane/ We're untouchable touchable girls': singers, Linda and Jools Topp. 'We have a lusty passion for women': writer, Miriam Saphira.

If men were the enemy, sleeping with them, letting them penetrate and possess you, was the ultimate collaboration. Feminism by the eighties was fraught with sexual division. Lesbians had battled from the beginning for recognition. The feminist movement learned new words—heterosexism, prejudice against people on account of their heterosexuality; homophobia, fear of homosexuality.

But the labels could mask genuine anguish.

> Feminism not only suggested women could have value apart from their sexuality, it provided a place—the women's movement—where you could have value. One of the things I really resented about lesbianism was that it sexualised the women's movement and brought in the tensions of the sexual marketplace. Women started eyeing each other up. I remember one of my closest friends making a pass at me. When I didn't respond she bad-mouthed me and said I was homophobic.
>
> And some lesbian behaviour mimicked what I didn't like about men's behaviour. I once heard two lesbians talking about the woman who lived next door to them and it was like a couple of truck drivers talking. They had a predatory attitude: all women were lesbian and they would help us discover it.

Not that everyone cared: 'Lesbians used to joke about who would get me first but it didn't worry me. I just shrugged it off.'

Feminism promised a place where you could have value, whomever you slept with. Its sexual effects were personal, idiosyncratic and often intense.

> I eventually came to feel that there was a deeply ambivalent problem in being a committed feminist and sleeping with a man. I know people have developed rationales which are more or less satisfactory, but I couldn't, and I began to withdraw from relationships with men. The sort of thing I tolerated when I was young—hop into bed, whip it out and have it away—I just could no longer endure. I had to have a long softening up period before anything like penetration could occur.
>
> I decided the only thing that would make me feel okay as a feminist was to be a lesbian. But that's got nothing to do with feeling I could never sleep with men. I could sleep with them tomorrow. Lots of lesbians say they've always felt lesbian and they could never bear anything else but that's not me. With me it's philosophical and political.
>
> I personally think it's impossible to have equality in heterosexual sex at the moment because even if you were lucky enough to find a man who was a true feminist (as far as men can be feminists), this man will nevertheless be supported by a huge structure in society that gives him more. And I would always be enraged by that. Anywhere you go you're going to be treated as the wife or partner or girlfriend of that man.

Lesbian sexuality initially had the power to shock—feminists as well as the world. Seventies books such as Jill Johnston's *Lesbian Nation* and Shulamith Firestone's *The Dialectic of Sex* proposed it as not just an option but *the* option, the only true way. Sexual correctness had torn at the heart of the feminist movement. Somewhere towards the end of the eighties, though, anger and argument had given way to a strange feeling of peace. Not resolution of sexual differences (probably unachievable) but accommodation—to each her own, and the shared understanding that sex of any sort is difficult—tender, orgasmic and (yes, Germaine) even, from time to time, ecstatic; but all too often painful, compromising or just mechanical.

At the beginning of 1993 Pamela Stirling reported in a *Listener* cover story that more and more heterosexual women were finding penetrative sex unsatisfactory and saying so. She quoted Fran Ginivan, a family planning counsellor, saying:

The problem is that female sexuality has always been defined by a male sexual norm. For women there may be equality in all areas of their relationship in terms of career and money and stuff, but in the bedroom he still expects to be dominant and it is seen as her duty to submit to his demands.

A new phrase was entering the liberation lexicon, sexual sovereignty—the right of women to have sex when, how and with whom they (the women) wanted. There was a new group of women who 'don't accept that men have a biological urge for release' and 'want partners who are interested in how to make a relationship work'—partners who, in Sheila Kitzinger's words, 'understand that feeling turned on for a woman on Saturday night starts at 11 am when he shares equally in the housework'.

From 1989 to 1991 Canadian journalist Wendy Dennis interviewed hundreds of women and men in cities from Vancouver to New York. In her book *Hot and Bothered* she wrote that the gulf between the sexes was widening alarmingly. Both men and women were repressing what they secretly thought and felt and needed in the cause of political correctness. Men no longer knew how to behave around women. If they tried to be New Men, emotionally sensitive, sexually unaggressive and good in the kitchen, women wrote them off as wimps. But if they came on the way they were expected to do in the good old days, they were likely to get kneed in the groin. And in their heart and loins, Dennis said, even the most ardent anti-sexist, female or male, still longed for 'the lovely primal edge sometimes engendered by those former roles'.

Lesbian women were also looking for the edge.

As a lesbian I find there is a preoccupation with the question of what happens after the first fine careless rapture, and why practically all lesbian couples find they can't sustain the sexual excitement. When this happened with men, we thought it was the politics and it would be perfect with women. So we're disappointed to find it's not.

There is a major difference though. In heterosexual relationships, if the sex goes off you tend to think there's something wrong with the relationship. In lesbian relationships, you can be very happy with the relationship but not be able to recapture the sexual interest even if both of you want to.

The strongest motif of sexual sovereignty in the nineties, though, was shaping up to be no sex at all. Not only had women of the sixties' generation finally found the confidence to say they weren't nearly as interested in sex as their male partners and never had been, but many were opting out altogether. A Gallup poll in England showed that given the choice of a hot bath, a drink or sex as a method of relaxation, women put sex a distant third.

The old maid of the sixties had become the by-choice celibate of the nineties. She probably owned a house with another woman, had a stimulating, well paid job, collected glassware, ceramics and antique rugs, travelled widely, studied Maori, and had friends of both sexes. One woman expressed it

> Feminism has freed me to look at my life and see what I need to be happy, without buying into the idea that it has to be a sexual relationship with a man—or, for that matter, a woman.
>
> I'm in my forties. I've been married. I've had an active sex life. I don't feel I have anything left to prove. I just find it a huge relief not having to deal with sex. I gave up the whole dating scene a few years ago. I'd been out with several people and it hadn't been a very positive experience. I'd examine whether I liked them, whether they liked me. It seemed rather adolescent.
>
> Women in our generation who are still having lots of sex are probably women who either don't find it very satisfying and keep trying to discover what the fuss is all about. Or they're desperately seeking intimate relationships and haven't found them. Men by nature aren't very good at intimacy. Women expect they'll get intimacy from sexual relationships with men but they rarely do.

For the women who entered sexual maturity in the sixties and seventies it was a disturbing, often disheartening and sometimes emotionally devastating experience. Most found that the generation of men they had grown up with were, as lovers, pretty much a lost cause. They had, as one of the men in Sue Kedgley's 1985 book *The Sexual Wilderness* rued, 'been brought up all wrong'. Jim, 49, related how during the breakdown of his marriage he saw sex with his wife as something akin to Custer's Last Stand:

> I began to count the nights when it happened. I'd say to myself, this is the sixth night without it. It became an obsession. I'd sit at work and think, tonight's the night I'm going to strike.

Most of these men had a deep resistance to changing themselves. While women attended consciousness raising groups, read *The Women's Room* and examined their relationships, men seemed content to sit smugly in the sexual and emotional place occupied by their fathers and grandfathers. Even those who supported feminist goals, and did something about implementing them, seemed unable to change their sexual behaviour. Or at least that was how it seemed to women desperate for signs of a breakthrough.

The truth, though, was probably more complex. In a moving essay in Michael King's 1988 book *One of the Boys?*, writer Kai Jensen described how difficult he had found it, as a male, to break away from the habits of the past.

> I have found that regarding most women as potential sexual partners, no matter now unlikely or potentially destructive the pairing, is a durable habit . . . To make it harder, we are surrounded by images which tell us that women exist for no other reason than to be alluring to men—that sex is their purpose.

Of sex itself he wrote that orthodox intercourse was a cause of increasing discomfit.

> Rapid, aggressive strokes of my penis may help me keep up my level of desire and excitement . . . But I feel uncomfortable with the aggressiveness of these movements; they suggest to me that I am, as slogans of the women's movement maintain, a potential rapist.

It is probably significant that Jensen, born in 1959, was still a child during the sexual revolution of the sixties and was, to boot, not born here but in the United States. Certainly few New Zealand men of the previous generation had subjected their sexual behaviour and expectations to the sort of scrutiny he had.

For Jim, in *The Sexual Wilderness*, sex was a battleground, a power struggle, 'the one area where I wasn't in control except for a few seconds or minutes'. At the heart of the matter was a deep male fear of losing control, independence, being taken over by a woman. During sex the penis, the archetypal image of male power, could be swallowed and concealed.

For women, too, sex conjured up primeval fears: penetration, wounding and capture—fears stoked by the hostile language used by men to describe the sexual act. Men rarely made love. Mostly they rooted, poked and screwed. Sex was not an act of equality but something you did to a woman who, whatever she said or however she protested, would love it in the end.

Feminism, however hesitatingly, challenged the male-controlled bedroom. Gains in other areas had a curious effect: showing up how little had changed in the most intimate sphere of people's lives. By the nineties, the disparities had become impossible to ignore. Sex would be the last testing ground of the revolution. Two things made change imperative. One was the factor identified by Wendy Dennis—the widening gulf between what women and men wanted sexually, and were prepared to deliver. Ninety-two percent of women didn't climax during intercourse—and more and more they were prepared to say so. The fake orgasm was rapidly going the way of the high heeled shoe and electrolysed armpit.

Women were also prepared to say that sex without tenderness was a turn-off, and that they were more likely to be aroused by a man who shared the housework and took the kids out than by one who fumbled inexpertly with their clitoris after an afternoon overdosing on telerugby. If male-female relationships were to survive, men would have to come to the negotiating table.

The other even more pressing catalyst for change was HIV/AIDS. It was not entirely sensible to accept a submissive sexual role when your life could be at stake. Suddenly it was hardly possible to open a women's magazine without encountering explicit sexual material of the sort that 20 years before would have had the Customs Department reaching for the fire-thrower. *More* magazine advised its young, credit card-carrying female readers not just to insist their male lovers used condoms but to demand two clean HIV tests three months apart before getting into bed in the first place. *Next* magazine detoured from its fables of motherhood over 40 and make-it-yourself duvet covers to warn women they were twice as likely to catch HIV/AIDS from infected men than men were to catch it from infected women, and that the risk was greater when they were menstruating. The *Woman's Weekly* ran a sympathetic story in which prostitutes argued for decriminalisation to help prevent the spread of the disease.

Suddenly, plain talk from women about sex was not just acceptable, it was startlingly fashionable. Stirling's article in the

Listener, 'Sex: After the Revolution', was mirrored in numerous overseas magazines. An international wire service flashed the news that not only was lesbianism again the rage in London society as it had been between the wars, but that this time women were openly flaunting it. Vanessa Feltz in the British glossy *She* decried the

> misguided prudery which depicts ordinary people's ordinary sex lives as too debased and animal-like to be referred to in public. . . . Boobs and bums may be in the public domain, but referring to whether or not most women enjoy sex during menstruation emphatically isn't.

The sexual openness was flushing out more than female angst in suburban bedrooms. American journalist Gail Sheehy, after writing a book on female menopause, decided male menopause was a much more common and dire problem. Many middle-aged men, she reported, had difficulty getting and sustaining erections, lost sexual desire, and without an understanding partner could become impotent. But not to panic. It could be a time for them to pause and reconsider the narrow identity by which they—and society—had defined themselves for the first half of their adult lives.

Walking on Eggs

DONNA AWATERE HUATA

MY STORY SHOULD BE SEEN IN the context of the struggle of Maoridom over the past century to regain control of our lives and destiny. The trauma of what Maori people had endured through our colonisation by the British came home to roost in my generation. We were the children of the soldiers who fought for the Pakeha, and of the parents who endured the trauma of the rural-urban shift. Our parents passed on to us their hurt and their sense of grievance. It was very much alive. So in a sense the role my generation played in trying to reclaim our tino rangatiratanga and take control of our destiny was set for us by our parents. They had sown the seeds of our uprising. All we needed was something to ignite our outrage.

My story is just one view of what happened. I became involved in the woman's movement because of a personal issue— my mother's right to equal pay. She was an egg packer at Egg Distributors in Wellesley Street in Auckland. I used to work there during the holidays and I noticed that my mother, who was a very fast and efficient egg packer, was paid less than the chap standing next to her, who was a slow egg packer. He got $20 a week more, simply because he was a man. It mightn't sound like much these days but her total pay was something like $37, so it represented an enormous discrepancy for doing exactly the same work. I brought the issue up with management and they claimed that it was because the chaps did other things such as lifting boxes. But the women lifted boxes too—and with no help, ruining their backs, while the men did it with a machine.

My mother shared my indignation about her pay but she hadn't been to school or had much education. She wasn't articulate in English, and her generation had a fear of Pakeha and a fear of authority that I hadn't learned. Most of the people in the factory were Maori and Pacific Islands and all the managers were Pakeha men. My mother saw the injustice of it, but she loved her work, she loved the environment, and she didn't want to change her job. In the end I got the sack from Egg Distributors. They said I didn't fit in.

When I was at Auckland University in 1969 the Equal Pay Bill came out. When I read the Bill and realised that it would never ensure my mother equal pay, I decided to go along to a meeting about the Bill. I was one of two strangers who turned up; the other was Sue Kedgley. I was nervous about being there but thought they talked a lot of sense. There seemed to be a lot of men there, and the fact that men could be passionately interested in the issue of equal pay—in whether my mother was treated fairly—seemed to me a very good thing.

I hadn't thought of myself as a feminist and I'd never read anything feminist, but I found I was on the same wavelength. I hadn't been brought up to think I was a lesser being, or that someone ought to get more money or better treatment than me simply because of their sex. I had a high level of self respect and when people didn't treat me with the same level of respect I'd received as a child, I was very annoyed.

There was so much happening in the early seventies that I soon found myself operating on many different levels. In the Maori arena I was spearheading issues in health, education and justice, particularly Treaty of Waitangi matters. At the same time all of us were having to defend ourselves in time-consuming court cases. I remember feeling incredibly stressed. My marriage had broken up and I was bringing up my two children on my own. But I had intensity, vision and total commitment. My mother and family were tremendously supportive. They buoyed me up emotionally and enabled me to give my energy to the cause.

Ngahuia Te Awekotuku and I were the most visible Maori women in the women's movement in the early days. We both took part in a women's liberation protest march to Queen Victoria's statue, where we laid a wreath and I composed a song, 'How much longer must we wait?' Shortly after that I began to get involved in Maori issues through Nga Tamatoa, the Maori protest movement.

I didn't see any conflict between the Maori and women's movements at first but as time went by this changed. I expected the feminist movement to be more understanding and supportive of Maori issues. Although I also felt that the conflict with men within the Maori movement was an issue Maori women had to sort out for themselves, and was not the business of Pakeha feminism.

I began to get put off Pakeha feminism by the way they trivialised their own issues. Consciousness raising was just recycling women's position. They would come to a session and have revelations which helped them manage their families and their relationships better, then move on without addressing the fundamental issues of women's status. One of the feminist mottos at the time was 'the personal is the political'. But most of the women didn't seem to make the political connections. They were obsessed with themselves and their own lives. We talked about things like how mean our partners were to us, but we didn't get on to the real issues like rape and incest and abuse.

In 1976 two Maori activists, Hilda Halkyard and Ripeka Evans, approached me to help re-form Nga Tamatoa, which had lost its energy after the 1975 land march. The old leadership, people such as Hana Jackson, Ted Near, Val Irwin and Linda Smith, were exhausted. No men wanted to join so we ended up as an all-woman group by default. Naturally we looked at women's issues and attracted more women members. Until this time nobody in Nga Tamatoa had had a feminist perspective. Hana had stood up and spoken on the Waitangi marae but she hadn't articulated a feminist philosophy. We decided that sorting out our men was high on the agenda.

122

We had already challenged men who had Pakeha partners at a hui in Wellington. We said, 'If Maori is so great, how come Maori women are not so great? Why did you select Pakeha partners?' I remember a sculptor standing up and saying he would slit his wrists and draw blood for the struggle. He made a blood-drawing movement on the stage and I leapt to my feet, rushed to the front and said, 'You hypocrite, you'd spill your blood for the struggle but you spill your sperm into a white woman every night.' That went down like a ton of bricks. Even the women were embarrassed: you just didn't say things like that. I used to talk like that—'pump your sperm'. I deliberately set out to shock so the men would see they were hypocrites. They had been conditioned to think Pakeha women were better. One way of annexing capital has always been to marry it. And they had the idea that there was a high in going with Pakeha women that they wouldn't get with Maori women. I felt very strongly that if they couldn't see the beauty in Maori women, and see us as partners, we were lost. It was particularly annoying that many of their Pakeha partners were quiet and submissive women. If they had been more fiery and supportive of us, I might have felt differently.

We were also concerned about the need for child care, about abortion, women being beaten, and the way we were treated as activists by Maori men. I would be in the back of the organisation writing the press releases and speeches but I'd never be up front. Hana, who was a brilliant organiser, was never given credit for it. The men always voted in dingbrain male executives who were ineffective and seemed to be bombed out on dope. They were wonderful speakers but hopeless organisers.

Women's right to speak on marae was also an issue at the time, but not one I felt strongly about. In some tribes it's a longstanding tradition that women are not allowed to speak. In others it's fairly recent. Ngati Porou, for example, always used to have women speakers. Now they don't. But I accept that as one of our rituals, and I feel sentimental about our rituals. They've been shovelled about enough. For me the Treaty was and still is the number one issue. It took all our energies in the seventies to shout and scream it into the position it has today.

I went to the United Women's Conventions in 1975 and

1977. They were festivals, celebrations of the work we did as feminists, and I found them spiritually refreshing. I wasn't bothered by the yelling matches, and by the lesbian faction bringing out the knives and everyone fighting. I was used to it on marae. That was family. You got together and had fights; it was half the fun. It did bother me, though, that Maori women were marginalised at the conventions and we protested about that.

Then in 1979 I went to a the white women's hui at Piha where the dykes and the hets split. It was a tremendously volatile and intense occasion. The split had been building up for some time: you can't achieve the kind of changes we were after without that intensity of feeling.

Sandra Coney stood out as a beacon of common sense through it all. She was attacked in a way few could have withstood but she stood her ground. She kept saying that everyone had a role to play, and that there was nothing wrong with heterosexuality. She did not accept the guilt that many lesbians wanted heterosexual women to feel. She was the only one who kept her cool and was courageous enough to keep standing up and speaking. It took a lot of guts. We became really close friends after that. I bonded with her courage in withstanding such an emotional battering.

Nobody attacked me at the hui, because as Maori women we were on the moral high ground, we were trebly oppressed. In 1978 I had had a car accident so I was badly scarred at the time. I had a mutilated face and was blind in one eye—which made me quadruply oppressed! Ngahuia Te Awekotuku and I gave speeches attacking Pakeha feminism. We said that we had allied with Pakeha women on feminist issues and they should ally with us on Treaty issues. Sandra Coney was the only one who didn't resist this. We had spent so much time together getting plonked that she started looking at the issues and taking them on board.

I think the reason the Maori movement flourished through all the feminist warfare was because we had very strong support systems and we had hui. We find it hard to leave our hui until everyone's healed; whereas Pakeha women seem to put the knife in and walk out. They don't take responsibility for what they've done to one another.

In 1979 Ripeka, Josie Keelan and I were asked if we wanted

to go to Cuba for the anniversary of the Cuban revolution. When we came back Robert Muldoon then Prime Minister called us Cuban-trained urban revolutionaries. The experience did have an impact on us, although not the one they thought.

When we got to Cuba, there were 18,000 other visitors. We were accommodated 50 miles away from Havana with the Americans, Canadians, Australians and New Zealand Pakeha, and we never got to see Fidel. But then we had a lucky break. A Palestinian had been shot in Paris and his body had been brought to Cuba because the PLO were there. We decided to go to the tangi. We dressed in black and put green around our hair, then we waited at the gate, and when the hearse arrived from the airport we did a karanga. Ripeka gave a speech in Maori and we did a haka and a waiata.

From then on we were identified as special people. We were invited into the palace where we met the survivors of the Palestinian hijack team, who were all women. I have a picture of the colonel embedded on my brain. She had lost her mother and all four of her daughters in hijackings. She went around in army fatigues and boots, with grenades and guns with bullets hanging down. I had never even seen a gun before.

We met liberation movement people from all around the world and this really changed our views. The women we spent our time with were freedom fighters and had their own mana. All that had ever happened to us in New Zealand was being arrested and getting worn out. No one close to us had died. When we came back we took our struggle a lot more seriously and had a lot more anger towards people who wouldn't acknowledge the importance of the Treaty.

In 1980 Nga Tamatoa—really by this time Hilda Halkyard and me—called the first national black women's hui. We were intolerable. My husband says he can't bear to look at the photographs because I look so arrogant. But the arrogance was necessary—it kept us going.

When it looked as though the Springbok rugby tour would go ahead, I pushed my way on to the national committee against it and Ripeka got on the Auckland committee. Nga Tamatoa had a big presence in Auckland. We used to go to hui and talk in Maori about the tour and the Treaty. Through Patu Squad and other activities we shifted the debate out of South Africa and back home.

I got arrested a number of times and faced some very serious charges, such as riotous destruction, which carried seven to 14 years imprisonment. I was supposed to have caused two million dollars worth of damage on one charge and one million dollars worth on another, as well as breaking a policeman's collarbone. The guy was six foot four: I couldn't even reach his collarbone, let alone break it. We decided to defend ourselves in court which was very stressful. We were also under financial stress and on top of that I had another eye operation, about my sixth since the accident. I spent two weeks at home convalescing and the pain was incredible. I started thinking, 'What are we doing? Where are we going? Should we have taken part in the Springbok tour? What are our objectives?'

I sat down and poured all my thoughts into an article about Maori sovereignty. I wrote it and didn't think any more about it until one night when Sandra Coney came round to dinner. We started arguing about Maori issues and I said, 'Hang on, I'll go and get this thing I've written.' It was very rough but Sandra asked whether she could publish it in *Broadsheet*. She took it away and edited it into three articles which *Broadsheet* published in 1981 and subsequently as a book.

My article on Maori Sovereignty was important because of its impact in Maoridom. It articulated a lot of vague feelings Maori people had. We were all involved in so many issues we were losing sight of what the struggle was really about. The book centred debate on the Treaty and the question of separate development, and addressed a lot of questions such as whether we ought to become more assimilated. I said we shouldn't. At the very least we should question the direction in which we were headed.

I went numerous hui after the article had been published and didn't get any hostile reaction from Maori. The hostility came from Pakeha people who said Maori couldn't stop howling about how bad things were and wanting their land back. None of this affected me at all. I'd be more worried by that sort of reaction now— although only because of how it might affect our business. But in those days I felt strong and I had constant daily support from my family. They didn't understand what I was on about but they had faith in me. They said, 'If Donna says that, it must be right.'

Robert Muldoon treated me very meanly. When at the end of the seventies he announced a list of New Zealanders he considered dangerous subversives, I was at the top. I got seared into people's memories as one of the causes of the worst violence of the Springbok tour. I spent most of 1982 and 1983 in court. When the first three charges against me came up, my lawyer Rodney Harrison put up an excellent defence, but I was convicted. I found this especially galling as they were the only charges of which I was truly innocent. After that I thought, 'Bugger that, I'm going to defend myself. Justice stinks.' And I got off all the rest. In one case I was up with four other people and all of them went to prison for over two years. I was the only one who was let off. I didn't want to go to prison. I had two young children and a lot to achieve.

After the Springbok tour the relationship between feminists and Maori changed. The Zeitgeist was right for Pakeha women to start looking at Maori issues. We always knew instinctively that Pakeha women would support the Maori struggle because women have empathy. We see it in the anti-racism courses our company runs now. The men will clear their throats when they read a Waitangi Tribunal report, but the women will often stand there with tears running down their faces. And afterwards they will try to bring a Maori dimension into the work they do. Men find it more difficult.

In 1984 I went into business, almost by accident. I had been looking for a husband for some years. The biological clock was ticking and I wanted some more kids. Eventually I found the husband I wanted. The night I met him he said, 'What's the key issue facing Maoridom?' I said, 'White racism,' and he said, 'No, you're wrong. The key issue is unemployment because when a family is unemployed they've got no money, they become flunkies of the state and they lose their independence.' He asked me whether I'd ever been out of work and I said I hadn't. He said, 'Who should create work for Maori?' and I said, 'I suppose Pakeha because they've got all the resources.'

'No, not Pakeha,' he said. 'If a Pakeha can choose between a Maori and a Pakeha for a job, which one will they choose? The

Pakeha. So who's going to help Maori unemployment?'

I said, trying to get the right answer, 'Maori people?'

He said, 'Absolutely. And who in Maoridom have got the resources to do it? Have you got a home?'

'Yep.'

'Have you got a car?'

'Yep.'

'Have you got a job?'

'Yep.'

'How much do you earn?'

I told him.

'How many degrees do you have?'

I told him.

He said, 'Then you're the one who should be doing it because most people haven't got those advantages. With your government job, you're no better than a flunky of the state. I would never work for the state.'

I thought, 'God, this man has no respect for me because I'm a flunky of the state.' So the next day I went to work and said to my partner, 'We'd better go into business and try to create some employment.' We handed in our resignations and left two weeks later.

We had been on high salaries as qualified psychologists and we had no idea what we were going to do. I knew nothing about business plans or marketing concepts. I had to take out a mortgage of $30,000 on my house because we went broke. We spent three months trying to sell, but without much idea of what we were selling or whom to sell it to.

We were trying to sell anti-racism training but in those days you couldn't give it away. In the end we were taken on by the Department of Justice. The work we did for them was lucrative and after 18 months we could see a need to raise the awareness about Maori issues among senior public servants. We formed Ihi Consultants and never looked back.

In the beginning we were a little ostentatious. The minute I got some money I bought an Alfa. Then we bought an office building, farms and houses, and all our family did well. We'd go overseas three times a year and take the whole family. I had always had a high standard of living. My pay as a psychologist had gone up every year. I lived in a beautiful two storey, four bedroom tudor house with kauri woodpanelling and had a new car every few years. What changed now was my level of disposable income.

When I got together with my husband in 1984 (we got married two years later) I'd been a sole parent for 13 years. I had breastfed my children, one for five years and one for three (my children now only get breastfed for two years). I had been able to focus totally on Treaty issues without any responsibilities to a husband or partner. But I wanted a close relationship. I wanted to grow old with someone and have more children, and I had to have a man for that.

I recently read Susan Faludi's book *Backlash*. I don't agree with her that there are new forces massed against women. The forces she talks about aren't new—they've always been there. In fact men used to resist change much more stridently than they do now. Now at least they're polite about it. It's no longer so acceptable to run women down.

It is true that women are still assimilating into a predominantly male culture, but we do bring our own qualities into the workplace. The only government department that has approached the bicultural issue in a revolutionary way, for example, is the Ministry of Transport headed by a woman, Margaret Bazley. Yet Margaret Bazley is not a charismatic leader. She is just a brilliant communicator with a very womanly style. When Beverly Wakem was head of Radio New Zealand, she was the best communicator of any chief executive I met. Her abilities were outstanding and she brought womanly qualities into her work.

On the other hand, there are plenty of women who aren't like this, who quickly get acculturated to the mean-spirited, individualistic, competitive, male environment of many organisations. I regard them as sleepers. It's the same with Maori. A Maori may act like a Pakeha through most of their career, but when they get somewhere they can make changes it's amazing how Maori they become. People say they're born-again but I look on them as sleepers who didn't have any options. When they do, they act differently.

Maori want to create Maori-friendly environments in organisations and women want to do the same. When you get a lot of women working together they tend to create a unique environment. I have run many courses which have been almost all women, and the way they behave and relate to each other is quite different from the way men do. I've noticed that experience tends to radicalise women. A woman who's been in the Treasury A team for a long time may have a baby and suddenly find herself in the D team. A few knocks like that can be very liberating. And I find that even women who act in male ways still have a womanly side which is ready to be reconnected with other women—that part of themselves that isn't competitive and individualistic; the healer and the nurturer.

I feel for women who opt for the male way, just as I feel for Maori who go Pakeha. They have to become something they're not, and there's a lot of pressure to succeed and become managers and role models. In my own case, when I look back on my 11 years working in the Department of Justice Psychological Services, I'm amazed that I didn't leave earlier. I had bought into the white male culture. I struggled harder than most, and was suspended from my job several times, but I capitulated to the salary and the security and the respect of colleagues. I should have left after a year—that's one of my few bitter regrets. One of the things I do now is help young Maori women leave, whether it's relationships or work situations. I found it easy to leave my first husband because I had economic prospects, confidence, heaps of resources and support. Although he was wealthier than I was, I wasn't tempted to hang about. But many women's options are very limited. It comes down to self esteem and self respect.

The public perception of Maori women is dominated by statistics—we are under-employed, under-achieving, over-imprisoned, over-offending. But I see it differently. Maori women have many opportunities which Pakeha women don't have. We have management opportunities through marae management and organising huge hui. Hundreds of ordinary Maori women have started kohanga reo from nothing, for example. They have fundraised, done the lot. There's still a lot of work to be done to raise the economic status of Maori women and see that girls are less damaged by abuse in their upbringing. But the fact that so many survive it and go on to play an active role in running Maori society is a cause for hope.

Maori women have made stupendous changes over the past 20 years. They now have opportunities that were never open to my generation of women, and they have very different expectations. Their attitude to their men has changed, for example. Most have an expectation—whether it's met or not—that men will help bring up the children and share the housework. That expectation wasn't there 20 years ago.

Maori women have another advantage too. Most Pakeha women seem to be isolated individuals who exist on a little island that involves their husband, their children, perhaps their parents, uncles and aunts and a few cousins. That's all they've got, whereas Maori have a sense of responsibility to the past, to new generations, to relationships they can have with their environment, to a spiritual dimension. We also have extended relationships. Just being Ngati Porou, I can go to a Ngati Porou hui and immediately there are 18,000 people who support me because I'm from the same tribe. I have an automatic support system.

That's one of the reasons why Maoridom is such an unstoppable force. We know what we want, we think alike, and we support each other. Whenever you have a group who think the same way they have an enormous power. That's why I am confident we will reclaim our own mana and our right to manage our own destiny. We will also become the leaders of the nation and fill the vacuum within Pakeha society.

I am optimistic about the future. I see New Zealand as one canoe. We're all in it together. If we can't get it together here, in our small society, then who else in the world can?

A New Breed of Women

FIONA KIDMAN

I ONCE SAT IN A ROOM FULL OF aspiring women writers and listened to an academic poet from Auckland University tell us how to write. He placed his hands on the table in front of him and intoned: 'Lady writers, eh? A nice little hobby. Now would you like to hear what real writers do?'

So there it was. Men's work was real, women's a hobby.

The views of the speaker, Kendrick Smithyman, were, as it happens, already known in some circles. In 1962 he had written an article for *Mate* magazine about post-war New Zealand poetry, in which he said: 'To say that in recent years the women who deserve to be called poets appear more intelligent is to sound superior; I do not mean to sound so any more than I mean to be ambiguous about the advances which women poets have made, but alas, not to me.'

It is nearly 30 years since this happened but I still remember how stunned I was. I wanted to be a 'real' writer. I was ready to commit my life to paper. I had begun to understand and come to terms with the solitary nature of the work. But I was 24, I lived in the suburbs of a provincial city, and what I did was often considered odd, or unwifely.

Yet some worthwhile things did happen to me in that long ago week in Auckland. I found, for instance, that other apparently quite ordinary women also wrote. What I did secretly, furtively, often in the early hours of the morning, was not as disgraceful as I thought.

Nevertheless, I was convinced that I was unworthy to take a place in the world of letters. I still wanted to write but I decided to aim at a modest level. I went home to Rotorua, retrieved my child from the minder, and got on with a bit of journalism for the *Woman's Weekly*. I published an article called '21 Ways to Make Money at Home' which featured on the *Woman's Weekly* billboards and I earned 20 pounds. I thought I was made. As well, many women told me how important and useful they had found the article. My confidence slowly began to recover, although later I would learn that 'popular' writing was 'trivial'. The words 'popular', 'down-market', 'ordinary', 'domestic', would come to haunt me.

I began to write at a time when it was very difficult for women to be acknowledged as serious writers, even though four times as many women as men admitted to a serious desire to write. The situation is still much the same. Christine Cole Catley, one of my predecessors at Victoria University's University Extension courses (now the Centre for Continuing Education), alerted me when she wrote: 'Women, who outnumber men by four to one in workshops, often have a driving need to practise setting down a story which is particular and peculiar to being a woman.' I have taught creative writing courses for 16 years and have found this to be true almost without exception.

In 1993 New Zealand women's writing looks healthy. Nearly half the books published are by women. In Keri Hulme, Lauris Edmond and Margaret Mahy we have writers who have won major international literary prizes, against male and female competition. The tragedies which beset Janet Frame as a young writer, her years of misdiagnosis and incarceration in a psychiatric hospital, have become the stuff of legend and the big screen in a film called *An Angel at My Table*, based on her autobiography. Barbara Anderson, who began writing in her late fifties, won the 1992 Goodman Fielder Wattie Award and unstinting praise from international critics for her novel *Portrait of the Artist's Wife*. The

Queen Elizabeth II Arts Council Literature Programme now supports women in fair ratio to men, and the bookshops are well-stocked with anthologies of our work.

Nobody should be misled into believing that these achievements have been easily won.

The nature of women's writing is that of story telling itself. From out of the deep and secret places within us, we weave the fabulous and magic mysteries that we tell our children, we retell old myths and legends and re-create the world anew for each generation. We spin the yarns of love so that our lovers may believe in our dreams, we tell each other what the truth really is when the dreams come unstuck. Those stories are told over fences, down the telephone or, if we are modern women, through the fax machine and in the women's room. As writers we record those stories so that others may read them and say to themselves, yes, this is it, this is what I understand, this is how it has been.

Yet 30 years ago, the writing of New Zealand women was for the most part invisible, except for a handful of books written by women who appeared to have led, at best, lonely lives, at worst, tragic ones. I speak of women like Katherine Mansfield, Jane Mander, Robin Hyde, Jean Devanny, Sylvia Ashton-Warner and, of course, Frame. Detective writer Ngaio Marsh, based for the most part in Britain, was something of a law unto herself, not entirely perceived as a New Zealand writer, despite her contribution to local theatre. Poet and short story writer Helen Shaw (*The Orange Tree and Other Stories*) was one of the few writers with whom a young woman on the brink of a writing career could identify, had I but known of her; it was to be some years before I began to enjoy her support and friendship, through correspondence.

The reasons for this invisibility are not difficult to locate, leaving aside the views of Smithyman and his ilk. Knowledge, as Virginia Woolf discovered long ago, has been kept under lock and key by men. In New Zealand, our history is short, conspicuous for a strong Calvinist and missionary streak in the make up of our forebears, and for the need for womanpower on the land, and women to provide children for the rapid establishment of population. As Heather Roberts has indicated (in *Where Did She Come From? New Zealand Women Novelists 1862–1987*), women were required not only to provide domestic services but also 'a moral influence'. Education was the traditional preserve of men, who would run the affairs of state. Women who knew too much might not fulfil their obligations to a new society. In other words, a good woman got on with the job and held her peace.

But women are not easily silenced. Place a pencil and a shopping list in their hands, and the chances are they will turn the paper over and write a poem on it. The accumulation of experience in a new land could not easily be put aside. From the very beginning, women like Jane Deans, Lady Barker (otherwise Mary Anne Stewart) and Sarah Amelia Courage, recorded the essence of their lives in letters home, journals and diaries. The work of Barker and Courage was published last century, although fewer than 20 copies of Courage's book *Lights and Shadows* were published, and some of her friends were so offended by what they read of themselves that several of those were destroyed.

Fleur Adcock's sister, Marilyn Duckworth, began publishing fiction in the late fifties (the first was *A Gap in the Spectrum*, published when the author was 24); her fraught, funny domestic novels had much in common with the work of Margaret Drabble. Amelia Batistich had published *An Olive Tree in Dalmatia* in 1963, a collection of shining little stories about migrant experience. Then there was *Stand in the Rain*, Jean Watson's wonderful road novel, a response, perhaps, to the bush-whacking tales of her erstwhile partner, Barry Crump. True, the first edition of her novel was remaindered, while Crump's books have collectively sold more than an estimated one million, yet later editions of Watson's book have confirmed her enduring place as a writer who broke the huntin', shootin', 'blokes and sheilas' mould that dominated local literature.

In the early seventies perhaps the most tangible evidence of contemporary women's writing was to be seen amongst the ranks of the New Zealand Women Writers' Society. For a long time this group had encouraged a quiet but persistent body of publication. A lot of what did get published, it is true, was non-fiction of the comfortable or comforting kind, or fiction which fitted into patterns of reconciliation with the land and husbands. However, practical support was being offered to a new breed of writers, like Joy Cowley whose novel *Nest in a Falling Tree* appeared in 1967, a poignant tale of an unconventional love affair, and Margaret Sutherland, whose novels (*The Fledgling, The Love Contract*) explored domestic themes with a sometimes caustic pen.

Had it not been for the inspiration these women provided, I think I would have given up the dream of writing fiction altogether. They kept alight the notion that there were other truths, other tales to be told.

But change was in the wind in the early seventies. A more universal education system, the feminist movement and Germaine Greer's barnstorming visit to New Zealand, plus the handful of local literature that spoke with new and urgent power, were beginning to unsettle the silent majority. Sue Kedgley's book *The Sexist Society* and the establishment of the magazine *Broadsheet* by a co-operative that included Sandra Coney, Anne Else and Kitty Wishart, gave focus to local awareness.

My own life had begun to operate on several levels. In 1970 I had shifted with my family to Wellington. I needed an income, and the prospects for women's fiction didn't look rewarding. I began to write scripts for radio and later for television, encouraged by Bill Austin and Arthur Jones. After the deaths of both men I found myself working more or less alone in the field, and I had to foot it with men in the media in a way that I had not anticipated. I learned to drink, to say fuck and to stay out late at night. In short, I became one of the boys. Looking back, I don't much like what I see. Yet, at the same time, I was learning survival skills for staying afloat financially that have stood me in good stead ever since. A writer in this country has to learn to be versatile.

At around the same time, I met the poet Lauris Edmond. She was slightly older than I was, and had struggled against the odds, with a large family, to get a master's degree in English. We discovered a strong common bond. We both wrote poetry on the quiet. If fiction had seemed difficult, poetry had appeared an impossible goal to me. Still I doodled it late at night, like others draw pictures, on the edges of newspapers. Lauris wrote poems from deep within, about family, relationships, sorrow and joy, and later, as her life changed more dramatically than mine and a beloved daughter died, about loss and grief. This was searing personal writing, informed all the time by a total command of language. She was to become both a poet's poet and a people's voice; much later, her three volume autobiography (*Hot October, Bonfires in the Rain, The Quick World*) would speak of the same concerns to a still wider audience. In Lauris I discovered somebody with whom I could, for the first time, discuss the dilemmas of being wife and mother, writer and artist. The endless hours of talk, the long walks over the Wellington hills, the incessant phone calls to exchange news, hopes, plans to publish, began a new phase in my life. Before long, our poems began to appear in print.

Magazines like *Eve* and *Thursday* had been established in response to the growing demand for women's viewpoints and their content extended beyond merely homemaking information to include literary work. Their success may also have led to their downfall. The male editors of more general magazines, such as the *Listener*, began to publish more women's writing than they had in the past. Slowly the work inched into the literary periodicals. Book and anthology publication proved more elusive.

However, 1975, International Women's Year, was just around the corner. No story of the last two decades of women's writing in this country is complete without recounting the events of that year. In the words of Rachel McAlpine: 'the feminist movement was the trigger. We were all touched by it one way or another . . . it made women like me realise that we could and even ought to write.'

In the previous 10 years, only a handful of women's poetry collections had appeared, by poets such as Fleur Adcock, Ruth Dallas, Ruth Gilbert and Peggy Dunstan. But in 1975 no less than nine were published, six of them by first-time authors. Many of us believe that publishers who had ignored women's writing up until then suddenly decided, in a quite opportunist way, to jump on the bandwagon. Publishing books by women became the industry of the moment. My own collection *Honey & Bitters* was amongst books by a group of women that included Lauris Edmond, Elizabeth Smither, Rachel McAlpine and Christina Beere, all of us publishing books for the first time. True, Lauris and I held a joint launching for our books, at which Denis Glover, an opponent during the thirties of what he described as 'the menstrual school of writing', declared that 'lady poetesses should stay at home, mend the socks and be real housewives'. But, while Beere (now Christina Conrad) has become better known as a painter, the rest of us have continued to publish not only poetry, but short stories, novels, and non-fiction.

It was at the International Women's Convention, in 1975, that the combined energy of women found its voice. The convention was held at the Wellington Show Buildings over a weekend of torrential rain. While the rain all but drowned out some speakers, thousands of women were forging bonds. I was a speaker, and to my astonishment I found that there were hundreds of women drawn by the word 'writer'. I stood on a wooden box and shouted. I recall little of what I said; I had had little premonition of the numbers of people and the scale of passion I would confront.

I learned more than I gave; for the first time I had serious discussions with lesbian writers and artists. At the original women writers' week in Auckland, I had asked a speaker about writing from different perspectives, such as lesbianism. Back came the reply: 'Why would you want to write about that at all?' Eleven years later, I was to engage in a dialogue which has gone on ever since. As I listened to lesbian women's stories and the difficulties they encountered, I learned that this was their story and not mine. But I found that there was room for active dialogue. I met the writer Heather McPherson who has been a central influence on lesbian writing and thinking for two decades. She was on the point of founding the feminist literary magazine *Spiral*.

Also planned for that year, but delayed for two years by publishing difficulties (ironically, the publisher was named Caveman Press), was an anthology of women's poetry, collected and edited by Auckland poet and peace activist, Riemke Ensing. When *Private Gardens* appeared in 1977, it was met with muddled responses from predominantly male critics. The troubling thing about this often raw and painful document was that it laid open the collective voices and griefs of women who had been silent, or silenced, all their lives. In her introduction Ensing wrote of the 'disturbing similarity' between the problems encountered 'in being a poet and a woman at the same time—problems which had to do with the *condition* of being a woman—of being a wife and mother first, a poet second.'

Janet Frame and Ruth Dallas both declined to be included in the anthology, on the grounds that a collection of women's work smacked of special pleading, thus opening a debate new to New

Zealand as to whether women's anthologies were valid. Janet Frame's denial of a female public appears to be something of a tragic irony. She speaks for women at the most extreme and radical level of consciousness, but appears alarmed by feminist debate. Perhaps her friendship with Frank Sargeson, and his coterie of young writers from around Auckland University, may have had some influence on her feelings. Sargeson had a reputation for generosity to the underdog, which Frame certainly was, when she went to live in his bach not long after leaving a psychiatric hospital, but his view of women writers in general was perhaps less expansive.

In this ferment of the mid-seventies, another significant change was unfolding. In 1976 I attended the first Maori writers' hui at a marae near Rotorua. I was instantly aware of a new mood of urgency amongst Maori writers. It was time, they believed, to write with their own voice, not to be heard through the voice of Pakeha. Witi Ihimaera had published the first ever works of fiction (*Pounamu, Pounamu, Tangi, Whanau*) by a Maori, to high acclaim. His achievements doubtless spurred others to succeed. J C Sturm had published a handful of stories in periodicals, starting in the fifties, but it was not until 1983 that her collection *The House of the Talking Cat* appeared.

Patricia Grace published *Waiariki*, a collection of short stories that made her the first Maori woman to publish a book of prose fiction. She says: 'My work [is] outside the "mainstream" of New Zealand work, because Maori people are a colonised minority in New Zealand society ... New Zealand is a multi-cultural society, but you wouldn't know this from reading our literature. ... That's why Maori literature has such an important place.' Grace has become one of the most powerful voices of our generation, her work anthologised all over the world. Her novel *Potiki*, about the threat of alienation of Maori land, won the 1987 New Zealand Book Award for Fiction. In her footsteps have followed Keri Hulme, the rumbustious poet/performer Bub Bridger, playwrights Renee and Riwia Brown, the poet Roma Potiki, whose collection *Stones in Her Mouth* is at the forefront of the new Maori publishing venture IWA, lesbian short story writer Ngahuia Te Awekotuku, the children's writer and publisher Mere Whaanga-Schollum.

In 1977 I began to write the novel I had long promised

myself. *A Breed of Women* was a frank story of growing up in New Zealand and what it was like for a New Zealand woman to develop a career and her creativity. It was published in 1979, and met with widespread critical hostility, dubbed by one male reviewer as the 'thinking woman's Mills and Boon'. Yet *A Breed of Women* caught on, and its total sales figures are now around 30,000. It was a particularly difficult time for me, especially as people identified so strongly with the character of Harriet Wallace that they wrote asking for personal advice and many believed that I had shared every one of her indiscretions. And, although I had worked in the media for a number of years, I had to learn now to cope with being on the receiving end of publicity, some of it adverse.

The most horrible incident occurred when I was scheduled to appear on a family entertainment programme. I sat for some hours plastered under heavy make-up, while the rest of the programme was pre-recorded. Finally my turn came. The compere didn't look quite like the Mister Nice Guy of the weekly screen. 'What about the morals of this woman, this character in your book?' 'What about her drinking?' he hammered at me. *What sort of example was I setting the women of New Zealand?* The audience laughed, titillated, as I was finally released to stumble away in the half dark over a pile of cables. I was refused a tissue to remove the make-up. Of course the item was never shown, nor, I realised later, had it ever been intended that it should. I was the comic turn, the extra. This unsavoury little tale graphically illustrates the way in which, at the most extreme end of the scale, men had decided to deal with women's experience, through calculated laughter and ridicule.

Again, after a period when I found it very difficult to write, there was a new woman friend from whom to draw strength. I embarked on a deep and important friendship with the poet Elizabeth Smither; her inspiration still communicates itself through my life and work. After a time, I began to write with confidence again.

By now the seismic tremors had turned into a wildly erupting volcano. Numerous women's titles appeared annually. Sue McCauley's novel *Other Halves* sold 24,000 copies and was made into a major film; novels by Joy Cowley and Anne Holden were made into international movies; on stage the playwright Renee packed out theatres with plays like *Setting the Table* and *Wednesday to Come*, which told of women's lives during depression and war; Anne French's powerful yet questioning love poems were finding their true voice (*All Cretans Are Liars, The Male as Evader, Cabin Fever*); Margaret Mahy was being published regularly in New York, and had twice won the prestigious Carnegie Medal for children's writing; Lauris Edmond won the Commonwealth Poetry Prize for her *Selected Poems*; Cilla McQueen was a joint winner with Allen Curnow of the New Zealand Book Awards Poetry Prize with *Homing In* (and has won the award outright twice since); Yvonne du Fresne, of Danish/French Huguenot extraction, was adding to the tiny body of ethnic literature in her stories about Jutland (*Farvel, The Book of Esther*); Meg Campbell revealed a powerful plangent poetic voice, and with her husband, the poet Alistair Campbell, set up the Te Kotare publishing house.

Promotion of women's writing appeared in the form of the Women's Book Festivals, organised on a voluntary basis by women publishers, editors, writers and booksellers, as well as book loving readers up and down the country. As well, Sharon Crosbie, the book loving host of the hugely popular morning National Radio programme, had introduced local women's writing into every far-flung corner of the country.

In 1984 the Spiral collective, begun by Heather McPherson, published Keri Hulme's *the bone people*. The following year it was reprinted by Hodder and Stoughton, won the Booker McConnell Prize, perhaps the most prestigious literary prize in the English speaking world, and sold more than 100,000 copies. The case for New Zealand women's writing, and Maori women's writing in particular, was made. Library borrowers and book buyers were being offered the richness of diversity and the stimulation of choice in their local reading matter.

But opposition lay in wait. In Canadian magazine *Ariel*, Auckland academic and writer C K Stead was writing that '*The bone People* [sic] touched New Zealand's currently, or fashionably, sensitive nerves'. New Zealand's intellectual life, he claimed was 'lacerating itself into a consciousness that racism and sexism exist'. 'Where they don't exist,' he wrote, 'zealots nonetheless find them. Keri Hulme, a woman and, let's say for the moment, a

Maori, her novel published by a "feminist collective" after being "turned down" by three others—this is the stuff for those zealots!' The energy which had caused the book to take off, he said, had 'nothing to do with the quality of the work'.

One of the more interesting features of this attack is that Stead chose to make it abroad. This has become a familiar pattern of attack by Stead against both Maori and women's writing, designed to fragment opinion and isolate the work from mainstream and international consciousness. His attack was some of the first tangible evidence of a backlash against the success and new-found acceptance of women's writing.

Hard on his heels came the voluble Michael Morrissey who has peppered many a letters column with his diatribes against women's writing. Writing in *Kite* (the newsletter of the New Zealand Literature Association) recently, he said: 'Increasing numbers of women in my writing classes tell me that they only read women authors. If this sexist tendency continues to spread male writers will obviously suffer.'

Mark Williams, a peripatetic English lecturer and critic, has carried the debate into the postmodern arena. Postmodernism, which works to overturn the conventions of traditional writing, rejects 'realist' writing. 'Realism' seeks to closely represent life, as it is lived, through literature. But women writing from the perspective of hidden lives, who want to tell 'truth' as they see it, usually write in a 'realist' mode. So, the argument goes roughly, women who write in a 'realist' mode are not as advanced as men who have passed through this 'truth-telling' phase and have now moved on to experiment in newer forms. Williams acts as a mentor to women whose work he perceives as experimental, and seeks to create schisms between them and other women writers, dividing them into one camp or another.

Of male mentoring, Adrienne Rich has written: 'Many women have known the figure of the male "mentor" who guides and protects his female student or colleague, tenderly opening doors for her into the common world of men.' But what, Rich asks, can he really bestow but the illusion of power? 'He can teach her to name her experience in language that may allow her to live, work, perhaps succeed in the common world of men. But he has no key to the power she might share with other women.'

This may be a terrifying concept, but it is at the heart of what drove the eighties backlash against women writers. Ultimately, Rich is saying, the power of women's writing lies within women themselves and what they know; not the forms or the fashions of the day, intrinsically interesting and useful as these may be.

None of this, of course, is to suggest that women themselves have been unaware of changes taking place in literature or unquestioning of the way they both write and define themselves. As Lydia Wevers wrote in an introduction to the short story anthology *Goodbye to Romance*: 'It is not just a question of bursting out of the frame, rewriting the self in opposition to the past, that is at work in the stories of women writers, but a more general destabilising of the boundaries which construct the gendered subject, calling into question all the terms which might presuppose identity: wife, mother, daughter, lover, woman, narrative, story.'

The last two to three years have seen a second wave of women's writing, following on the explosion of new writers and writing that took place in the late seventies and early eighties.

Elizabeth Smither, poet, short story writer and novelist, may well be seen as spearheading new developments which younger writers have followed. Her novel *Brother-Love Sister-Love* is a symbolic journey about European New Zealanders in search of their origins, as well as a picaresque view of marriage. Her poetic stance appears, on the surface at least, to be slightly detached, ironic, playful, and full of daring imagery. Of course, she is as much 'in' the work as any other writer, and the emotion is as keen as the next. But she also brings to bear a more observant and analytical eye than that of some earlier writers, describing not just how things are, but asking why; the answers are sought beyond self, whether they be grounded in the contemporary world, historical precedent, literary antecedents or the spiritual.

In her wake have emerged poets such as Jenny Bornholdt, Dinah Hawken (winner of the First Book division of the Commonwealth Poetry Prize for *It Has No Sound and Is Blue*), Bernadette Hall, Michele Leggott and Virginia Were. Their poetry tends towards the spare and experimental, but their concerns are still often intrinsically domestic, as in Leggott's celebration of motherhood. Bornholdt and Hawken frequently explore the correlation between art, life and literature, as does the novelist Barbara Anderson in her prizewinning book *Portrait of the Artist's Wife*. These three women, along with Were and novelist Elizabeth Knox (*After Z-Hour, Treasure*) could be regarded as the female focus of a movement of writers centred around Victoria University Press.

The use of irony is prominent in the work of fiction writers such as Sheridan Keith (*Shallow Are the Smiles at the Supermarket*) and Shonagh Koea (*The Woman Who Never Went Home, Staying Home and Being Rotten*). There is a sharp intellectual quality about their observations, an international flavour to their style which puts them in the forefront of good narrative story telling. Frances Cherry's novels (*Dancing on Strings, The Widowhood of Jackie Bates*) are quirky, laconic tales of sexual ambiguity both inside and outside marriage. Heather Marshall, like Barbara Anderson, began a prolific publishing career in her fifties, and writes convincingly of the Depression in *Second Hand Children*; Colleen Reilly is an American-born New Zealander who writes with fluid grace outside all the mainstream conventions of New Zealand writing. Her novel *Christine*, in particular, is a superbly crafted tale of a woman at the edge of society in a twinning role with a lost brother.

Political awareness of one kind or another shines through in the work of feminist poet Janet Charman and novelist and short story writer, Rosie Scott (*Glory Days, Feral City*). Charman explores her themes through nursing and hospitals—nothing could be further removed from the Sue Barton stories of my girlhood. Scott writes of the tragic alienation of the poor and of the uncertainty of the future, but also about the vicissitudes of love, in a rich, silky, sensuous prose which lifts her writing beyond polemicism. Scott and children and young peoples author, Caroline MacDonald, now live in Australia where both have rapidly moved to the forefront of their genres.

Fiona Farrell (*The Rock Garden, The Skinny Louie Book*) and Stephanie Johnson (*The Glass Whittlers, Crimes of Neglect*) are two more highly distinctive voices who have emerged in recent years. Farrell's prose is as dense and multi-layered as a patchwork quilt, charting the heart's course, but also revisiting women's pioneering past, while Johnson writes with sharp, edgy brashness of unglamorous lives and ordinary people whom she nonetheless perceives as important beings. Elspeth Sandys, Sue Reidy and Alice Glenday have all made significant contributions to women's writing; Janice Marriot and Christine Johnson (winner of the Reed New Fiction Award for her novel *Blessed Art Thou Amongst Women*) are writers of whom we will surely hear more in the future.

Women writers have had increasing support from publishing houses. Bridget Williams Books places a strong emphasis on women's writing, particularly non-fiction. *The New Zealand Book of Women* is an outstanding reference work of herstory, offering as it does over 300 biographical essays about the lives of New Zealand women. The emphasis of Daphne Brasell Associates Press is on women's writing. Their author Beryl Fletcher recently won Best First Book Award in the Commonwealth Literature Prize (South East Asia Pacific region) with her novel *The Word Burners*; it explores lesbian themes in a university setting. Fletcher had been encouraged in her early writing by Cathie Dunsford of Dunsford Associates, an editorial and publishing agency. New Women's Press published women's writing exclusively, and has published first-time writers such as Jacqueline Owen and Alexandria Chalmers, as well as writers whose work has become better known. Not that such commitment to women's writing is easy, even now. When Keith's collection *Shallow Are the Smiles At the Supermarket* was runner-up to the 1992 Commonwealth Literature Prize, New Women's Press managing director, Wendy Harrex said: 'That's the nearest any of my books have come to recognition since I began New Women's Press ten years ago. Yet I know my work is good. When I was a mainstream publisher, my books won prizes all the time. What's changed?'

The quietest success story, but perhaps the most significant in terms of women's self-determination, is to be found amongst writers for children and young adults. That I should leave them until the last does not reflect my view of their place in the order of things, but rather that in them I see hope for new endeavour and new beginnings for our daughters.

Writers such as Margaret Mahy, Gaelyn Gordon, Ruth Corrin, Sherryl Jordan and Tessa Duder write about strong, interesting, self-sufficient characters whose fortunes young women avidly follow and wish to emulate. Duder's *Alex* quartet traces the adventures of a young swimmer who, like the author herself, goes to the Rome Olympics. In the second book, *Alex in*

Winter, Alex has been fighting the odds as she prepares not only as a swimmer but also rehearses for a school play about Joan of Arc. She writes in her diary: 'When we got to the speech where Joan tells them to go take a running jump, the words are so beautiful and strong and defiant, something sort of took over. *Light your fire: do you think I dread it as much as the life of a rat in a hole? My voices were right.* I know Joan was talking about something much more important, like what she believes and how terrible it would be to be shut away in a prison breathing foul damp darkness forever, but, well, it's an amazing cry for freedom and life and it just came out . . .'

Women of the future may well come to writing with a greater sense of their own heroism and less of victimisation.

There is no space here to consider the vast body of non-fiction produced by women in this country, nor room to examine the contribution of a small but growing band of fine television and film writers. Instead, I have endeavoured, for the most part, to chart the development and expression of women's creative imagination in prose fiction and poetry. I began with my own story and moved to that of the broader writing community. For most women writers of my generation, I am sure that this is how the perspective of our experience has developed. We began from a sense of isolation and uncertainty, and moved slowly but surely towards some shared goals. I was astonished by how much grief and anger writing this chapter stirred up, how much opposition and denial I had to live again. But I have also been reminded of the joy that words and books have offered, the choices revealed.

The Corridors of Powerlessness

SONJA DAVIES

AT 68 I AM NOT THE WOMAN I was at 28 or indeed at 32 when I took part in the protest against the closure of the Nelson/Glenhope Railway and stood for the first time for a local government position. Certainly I'm not the woman I was when, quite unbelieving, I was told at the Federation of Labour conference in 1983 that I had comfortably won the ballot for the vice-presidency from the media supported favourite, the secretary of one of this country's most influential male-dominated unions.

It's no longer so common for a woman to be the only one on city councils, union executives or in parliament. But my main memory, when I look back at my local body experience as the only woman on a hospital board and a city council, is of acute loneliness, of not being part of the male club (heaven forbid) where so many decisions were made and presented at the next meeting as a fait accompli.

I remember a host of incidents common to women in positions of power. A request by me for justification or elaboration of the reasons for a particular decision taken in my absence would be met by exasperated sighs. While no one ever actually said, 'Don't worry your little head about it, dearie, we men know best', the implication was there and had to be challenged each time. I remember many occasions where I put forward a carefully researched idea to my male colleagues, and it plummeted like a damp squib. Several weeks later, a man would propose an almost identical idea, and everyone would applaud. I remember being told that I couldn't chair the works committee, even though I should have according to tradition, as I had topped the poll on Council. The men, I was told, would object.

At times like these I would wonder, 'If it was like that for me, what in heaven's name must it have been like for our pioneer sisters in parliament? What would they think about the women in parliament today, and about what women have done with the vote which they prised from the male hierarchy like an oyster from its shell? Have we kept faith with Kate Sheppard and her colleagues? Have we achieved what they envisioned in those fraught and courageous times?'

Sometimes I sit in the debating chamber when no one else is there, and think of the brave women who dared to breach this male bastion. We know how lonely Mabel Howard was, how no one would even tell her where the women's toilets were. I think of Whetu Tirikatene-Sullivan, my cousin, who produced two babies while she was an MP. But for her whanau support and her husband Denis, himself in a demanding job, how would she have managed? And of the situation that Ruth Richardson faced, wanting to breastfeed her baby in this alien environment where proper facilities were not available.

I think of Liz Tennet, whose son Matthew was born in her first term of office, and how she would have coped without strong support from her husband John and a nanny. Women MPs supported the parliamentary child care centre that Matthew now attends. But it closes at 5 pm. If, as must happen, more women enter parliament, good after school and holiday programmes need to be set in place, and the hours of parliament changed to cater for the needs of mothers, fathers and children.

I think of Marilyn Waring and the searing time she had. I used to see her knitting defiantly in the House. She was the first active feminist in parliament, and the first woman MP to challenge a lot of the National party's policies. When people realised how she had been treated, many said, 'This can't go on, we've got to do something to change it.'

But most of all I think of those first women MPs and ask myself what it must have been like for them. What was it like for Elizabeth McCombs, Iriaka Ratana and Hilda Ross to be part of such an unbalanced environment?

I stood for selection in Rotorua and Taupo in 1966, for parliament (unsuccessfully) in Hastings in 1966, and for selections in Nelson in 1978. I didn't have any female role models at the time but I'd always been political. I had the idea that this was where laws were made, and it was the only place where things could really get changed. I had also felt for a very long time that parliament was not a house of representatives because half the population wasn't represented in it. After losing two selections, I began to wonder whether it was because I was a woman, or because I was a stroppy person, who was promoting women at a time when there was a lot of prejudice against women who pushed for change.

When I was finally elected to parliament in 1987, nine years later, I realised how hard it is to change things. You're fighting on so many fronts and it's very lonely. It has also become obvious over the years that men will tolerate women in parliament only as long as they're prepared to accept the system as it is, and stick to non-threatening issues. When someone like Marilyn Waring tries to do things differently, the backlash is immense.

I hear women saying, 'Why have women in parliament at all, when they've achieved so little?' My response is, 'What's the alternative?' The alternative is a parliament of men making decisions for women, I doubt if that's what many women want.

Sixteen women in parliament is certainly paltry, considering it's a century since we got the vote, but I'm convinced that the more women we get into parliament, the easier it will be. There comes a point when you suddenly have enough people with you to push things forward (although we're not yet at that point—we need about double the number we have now).

Yet when I look back I realise that things have changed in the century that women have been in parliament, especially in the past 20 years. In 1972 there were only two women MPs, Rona

Stevenson and Dame Hilda Ross. Women were active in political parties, making the sandwiches and pouring the tea, but they were barely consulted on policy matters at all.

In the early seventies the women's report was always considered last at Labour party conferences, along with the Maori report. Most of the delegates had drifted off by that stage, and there were only a few left in the hall. A group of us were incensed by that, so we asked to move the women's report further up the agenda. We were told that wasn't possible so we organised a picket outside the conference, with placards saying we wanted justice for women. Labour cabinet ministers had to pass through the picket to get to conference. Needless to say, the report got moved.

Throughout the seventies, Labour party women fought through their branches, Labour electorate committees, the executive and council for recognition. Our goal was to get more women in parliament and in policy making positions in the party. I remember quite a few struggles with older women in the party, who didn't want to go that far. They were quite happy with their role, making cream cakes and sewing doilies and babies booties for fundraising. But we were a new group of women, very much influenced by the women's liberation movement, and we wanted to get better representation for women in the party and more women in parliament.

Germaine Greer had been in New Zealand and, inspired by her, we lobbied the executive for a women's officer in the party, and formed what was then called the Labour Women's Advisory Committee. We were full of hope and, in retrospect, quite naive. Like a lot of women, we had unreal expectations of what women in parliament could achieve. We had no idea how difficult it was going to be. We thought all we had to do was get into parliament and change would miraculously happen. We were convinced that women could do anything, and that the men were no better than us. All we wanted was a chance to prove it.

Women are listened to far more now than they were. We have quite a few younger male MPs who come from a different culture from the older MPs. They can actually hear what women have to say, and are capable of taking women's issues seriously. Give or take a few traditionalists, Labour women have a good relationship with our male colleagues, but it needs to be constantly worked at. There are conscience issues on which we sometimes part company, but by and large we have an understanding. It seems to me that National women have not yet reached that point, partly because they've never challenged the men in their party. They have had a woman president but I think even she was treated rather badly at times.

Women's issues have traditonally been considered 'soft', by the media as well as members of parliament, but that's changing. We're getting issues like child care, pornography and rape onto the parliamentary agenda. We have a small but powerful and supportive Women's Caucus Committee in the Labour party which meets every Thursday. It is hard for us all to meet each week, with speaking in the House, commitments and travelling out of Wellington, but we do support each other. We meet with women's groups like Plunket and Rape Crisis, and we decide on issues we want to debate in the House.

Until a few years ago, if women got together in a caucus, men would come up and say, 'What are you up to?' Men got together in huddles all the time, but when women did it was immediately considered suspicious. These days we can meet in a caucus without raising a lot of eyebrows and comment. On the other hand, when men wanted to come to our caucus meeting to hear what a group of women from Plunket had to say about the government's funding cuts, it made me realise how important it is that we have our own forum where we can discuss things without the men taking over, however supportive they may be.

One of the sad things for me is that we haven't had women's issues debated by women across the House in a non-party way. Sometimes Labour women will decide to hold a debate about a women's issue we consider important, such as rape or child care funding, but very few of the National party women will get up and speak about it. Instead some National fellow will stand up and say, 'Look, I want to talk about *important* issues like Gatt or the economy.'

Early on in my political career I realised and accepted that women have a different agenda from men, and different ways of looking at problems. I learned that things that matter to women, such as social justice, child care and care of the elderly, are considered worthy but not as important as, say, airport development, roading and parking facilities. In other words, they are soft options. Cabinet rankings clearly show where those options come in the male pecking order, although there are the occasional exceptions such as Minister of Finance Ruth Richardson, or Ann Hercus, who was Minister of Police, as well as Social Welfare and Women's Affairs.

Women coming into politics learn early that it's all about priorities, and that if there aren't enough of you in caucus, and enough sympathetic men to vote with you, the priorities will go the male way. For women in Cabinet, it's even more difficult. There are usually only a couple of women, both with quite weighty portfolios. It's a struggle just to get money for your department and survive as a human being when you're confronted with that volume of work. Even if there are two of you, you're working in different areas and travelling a lot, so it's hard to get together.

How many women, I wonder, have any idea of the hard work, tenacity and determination of Labour party deputy leader Helen Clark as she tried to push women's issues up the agenda? Many women who became critical and restive during what they saw as vacillation over the pay equity legislation had no idea of the strength of opposition from bureaucrats and, in some instances, male cabinet ministers. Helen Clark achieved a lot. She put women's health issues on the political agenda, gave midwives autonomy after 50 years of being handmaidens to doctors, and introduced anti-smoking legislation despite opposition from a vigorous and well funded tobacco lobby.

When the herstory of the Ministry of Women's Affairs is written, hopefully more people will understand that things like greatly increased funding for pre-school education didn't just happen by magic. Women such as Margaret Shields, then Minister of Women's Affairs, made them happen. Like a number of her woman colleagues, she could draw on her own hands-on experience with playcentres. And she fought constantly to have women's issues considered valid and important.

Parliamentary life imposes enormous strains on families. It contributes to failed marriages and disrupted family life. A woman needs a partner who isn't going to feel demeaned by

152

having a wife in parliament and by taking on some traditionally female caring roles. One of the most crucial issues we need to deal with is the effect on children, particularly teenagers, of having an MP or cabinet minister in the family. They are the ones who bear the brunt at school, in sport and elsewhere, and who become disenchanted when parliamentary duties stop their parents attending sports and cultural events and end of year prizegivings. There are so many times when you have to put the job first. A lot of people rely on you and you have to be there. Never mind if one of your children is off sniffing glue or deeply depressed. You're running all of the time.

There needs to be a major change—for men as well as women. Apart from former MP Trevor de Cleene, who has gone on record as saying that a backbencher's life is easy, most of us who are conscientious and hardworking know that the long hours in the House, on select committees, at caucus committees and weekly party caucus meetings, answering the prodigious mail, meeting electorate requirements, and travelling around the country to speak and meet people, and overseas to attend conferences, leaves little time for much else. Leaving home at 7.45 am and returning home at 1 am is not a recipe for good family life. For MPs with constituencies outside Wellington, who try to get home on Fridays, and have clinics and electorate responsibilities to deal with at weekends, quality family life is hard to attain. Former Labour leader Geoffrey Palmer brought some improvements, but women MPs now need to have an input into future changes.

I have no experience of knowing what it is like to be a woman in Cabinet, but my involvement in power institutions, local body, Federation of Labour and trade unions, and my discussion with past and present women cabinet ministers lead me to believe that it's far from easy. You measure up policies that affect women against a whole range of conflicting interests, and with at most one or two other women in Cabinet to support you.

Even so, women MPs travelling overseas are made constantly aware that we are well ahead of most other countries. In 1992 I went to Chile as opposition delegate to the Commonwealth Parliamentary Conference. At the women's meeting, we were given statistics showing that the number of women in parliaments around the world is actually decreasing, but that in New Zealand we have one of the highest—and growing—percentages of women MPs.

In 1986 I went to Australia with the select committee on Foreign Affairs and Defence to meet our counterparts and discuss common issues. The purchase of the frigates was in the negotiating stage, and opposition to it by some of us was seen by most Australian colleagues as unbelievably misguided. We were shown over the new parliament, the squash courts, the gymnasium, the shops, the bank, and I asked, 'Where is the child care centre?' The silence was deafening. This is a huge new building, built into a hill, with marble floors and wonderful artwork, including Aboriginal paintings. (I didn't see any Aborigines there, and even the cleaners were Maori, but that's another story.) When our hosts recovered from this strange request, they told me that there were facilities for changing babies in the spouses' room, so I asked to see them. The spouses' room was quite small and I was shown a cupboard in which was set a tiny bench and a sink, both obviously unused and impossible to change a child on. Later that day at a function, the then Prime Minister, Bob Hawke, buttonholed me, 'What's all this I hear about you stirring over here about us not having a creche?' I told him I was astonished that any government in the eighties could plan a new parliament as remote as this from the city, and with a large number of women employees, without including such an important amenity. He said (as though it explained everything) that if the government had provided one, employers would feel they had to. 'What's wrong with setting an example?' I asked. He excused himself and went off to talk to rational men.

For women coming into national politics, there are a number of lessons to be learned. The Westminster system we have was forged by men, for men, in that most male orientated powerhouse, the British parliament. It is bureaucratic, adversarial, wasteful of time and physical resources, and it produces minority governments. Geoffrey Palmer recognised that and made some changes. For me, the most important were the reforms of the select committee system in 1978 and 1985.

Clearly, we need another system. The Westminster system served us well for quite a long time, but its day has gone. The world

has changed and we have to change with it. But I'm not y
vinced that proportional representation will be the panac
harbinger of social justice that some of my women friends b
My friends in other countries with proportional representati ... ..,
that single interest people play the main parties off to get their own
way on particular issues, and that's destructive.

I don't believe the 1993 referendum on electoral reform will
be the end of the process of political reform. We're far too keen
on saying that what they're doing in other countries must be
good for us. We need to work out a parliamentary system that is
not British or European but designed to suit the needs of New
Zealanders. We've shed many of the trappings of colonialism.
There is now a fairly widespread awareness that we are a Pacific
nation with important links to South East Asia. The Treaty of
Waitangi, as the founding document of our nation, while it is still
suspect by those who either have not studied it or don't accept its
implications, is now something to be reckoned with when all
sorts of decisions are made. The resurgence of Maori culture and
language, and Maori's bid to educate their children themselves is
now an agenda item.

Women understand these changes to the fabric of our society.
It's when you get to the free market, user-pays philosophy that the
waters part for many of us. Why? Because when health and education funding and accessibility are reduced, and funds for community social services dry up, it's women who take on the burden,
as carers and nurturers of the young, the disabled and the frail
elderly.

Women work best when we are in groups, when we are able
to network together and know that there's a level of trust. We
don't work at all well in the new free market, go-it-alone, devil-
take-the-hindmost climate. That's why it was so difficult being in
parliament during my first term, from 1987 to 1990, when Roger-
nomics was at its height. Minister of Finance, Roger Douglas,
really believed in his economic philosophy, but I didn't. I couldn't
subscribe to a philosophy which destroys so many people's lives
to achieve its goals, so I felt very disenfranchised. I came in hoping there would be enough of us to change the government's
direction, but there wasn't. There were some good things happening, such as the introduction of better child care. But I would find

myself getting into the shower in the morning and hearing Roger Douglas or Richard Prebble, Minister of State-Owned Enterprises, on the radio announcing that Labour was going to sell off another asset, and that would be the first I had heard about it. Yet I was expected defend it to angry constituents. I expressed my opposition to what was going on inside the party, but I believe in party loyalty, so I didn't do so publicly. I believe you should keep your fights inside. If you don't have that feeling of being part of an organisation, even one you're not very happy with and want to change, you shouldn't be in it.

Despite some progress, sexism is alive and well within these hallowed walls, and ageism too. On my first day in the House, John Banks, who was then in opposition, called out 'Here comes Granny'. He continued to do this in the House and when he met me in the corridors. At first I retaliated but in the end I ignored him. This continued for several years but one day, when I entered the House for the beginning of the afternoon proceedings, the Leader of the House, Paul East, said 'Here's Auntie'. The iron entered my soul and when the Speaker arrived, and after the usual prayer, I rose to my feet and asked leave to make a personal statement. Permission granted, I said I was no longer prepared to put up with ageism, which I considered to be as invidious as sexism. I sought his support.

I hadn't had time to consult my colleagues but they supported me absolutely. I was also heartened by the women government MPs who came across to express their solidarity and to thank me for raising the issue. Then my old adversary, Sir Robert Muldoon, came over to me and announced, 'If you can't stand the heat, girlie, get out of the kitchen.' And, to my astonishment, he poked his tongue out at me. I remarked rather sharply, 'It's dirty, Sir Robert, you need Syrup of Figs', and he harrumphed and stamped off. I thought of this incident when he said, in his valedictory speech, that it had been hard for him to come to terms with more women coming into the House.

Men like Robert Muldoon had a fifties vision of Mum and home, the smell of bacon, and happy laughing children to whom they would come back after forays in the 'working' world. They would instinctively resist anything that might disturb this rosy vision—you can imagine how thrilled they must have been when feminists adopted the slogan, 'A woman's place is in the House of Representatives.'

If we look at parliament today, we see an establishment which is still male oriented, and dominated by the views and needs of the 80 elected men in it. The debating chamber, with its shields commemorating the various battles in which men have participated, says it all. There's nothing in the chamber to say that women have had any part in the fabric of our society at this level. The women who filled men's jobs during the wars, performing tasks no 'lady' had tackled before, driving trucks, working on trams and trains, in engineering workshops, on farms, and all of those who stayed at home raising families alone and still found time to roll bandages, knit balaclavas and socks, bake cakes for food parcels, which we now know were crucial to the troops' morale, are invisible here. Women's war effort remains unrecorded and unsung. So too does our struggle for the right to vote—until recently it was not even recorded in the New Zealand parliament, let alone in the debating chamber.

When funding for suffrage centennial year was proposed, there was an outcry in the male-dominated press, and extravagant statements were made about possible expenditure—an echo from the past. Some people were incensed that at a time of economic depression money should be spent celebrating the centenary of women's right to vote. From my clinics in Wainuiomata, Waiwhetu and Moera, I know very well the struggle that people have to survive, and my heart and energies are with them. But the centenary was so special that it could not go unmarked, and the amount allocated was a fraction of the GNP, and a sixth of that spent on the 1990 celebrations.

In the light of former British Prime Minister Margaret Thatcher and the unpopular policies women cabinet ministers have been responsible for in the Bolger National government, people say to me, 'You've always said that we need more women MPs, but look at these women. How do you feel about them?' My reply is that, even so, we do need more women in the House—more caring women who are closer to the people, and particularly to the women, they represent. For it is my strong belief that we will not have a real House of Representatives until it *is* representative. Women constitute half of the population, so they need to be there in that proportion, not only on a gender basis but on a racial one as well. Only then will we be able to come up with balanced policies which genuinely serve the women as well as the men of Aotearoa, and their children.

Lesbians
In Front, Up Front, Out Front

PAT ROSIER

GIL HANLY

DO NOT READ THIS AS A definitive herstory, but as an account of some of the activities, passions and ideas of a diverse 'obnoxious and unruly bunch' (after Sarah Hoagland in *Lesbian Ethics*) that became an identifiable group along with gay and women's liberation groups in Aotearoa/New Zealand from the early seventies. This is not 'the official history': there can be no official history of lesbians. There can be many items from many sources that together produce a kaleidoscope, a tapestry, a landscape, a 'lesbian body' (after Monique Witting) of work. In writing it, I have depended on hearsay. I risk giving offence by commission and omission. What is here is limited by my networks, the range of lesbians I approached who chose to respond.

This is a book about feminism. Stating the obvious: not all lesbians are feminist; not all feminists are lesbian. 'Sports dykes' are not here. Lesbians who have consistently worked in gay liberation need another history. Many groups of lesbians who do not identify themselves as feminist are not here either. Even the term lesbian feminist is problematic when referring to events

159

of the seventies. (Thank you *Bronwen Dean* for bringing this to my attention) 'Yes!' writes *Heather McPherson*, 'I was a lesbian separatist before I was a lesbian feminist. We felt feminists were suppressing/disowning lesbians to be more acceptable to patriarchs.'

There have always been lesbians, although lesbian is a word of the twentieth century. The herstory is as long as time itself and found in many lesbian writings, beginning with Saphho and more recently North Americans Judy Grahn, Joan Nestle, Julia Penelope and Lillian Faderman. In New Zealand women such as *Julie Glamuzina* and *Alison Laurie* have written of our recent Pakeha lesbian past; *Shirley* and *Ngahuia Te Awekotuku* have published stories of Maori lesbians.

Naming lesbians is a political act. If my source is a public one such as *Broadsheet*, if I have managed to find the woman and get her permission, or if she was publicly identified at the time as being lesbian, her name is used in full. If only her first name appears, it may be because her permission could not be gained, I could not find her, she did not respond to my asking, or she could not afford the disclosure: it can still be dangerous to be named as a lesbian in this country. In some cases there are only first names because that is all that was recorded or remembered.

This chronicle begins in 1973. Lesbians come out in Wellington, Auckland, Christchurch, everywhere, joining others who have been out as lesbians for years. *Alison Laurie, Sharon Alston, Marilynn Johnson, Ngahuia Te Awekotuku, Morrigan Severs, Porleen, Jan Smith, Maureen, Shirley, Janet.* A lesbian I correspond with about this article asks for her name to be removed from this list, because 'I didn't come out until 1974, though I'd had my first relationship in 1970 . . . and had a small lesbian group to socialise with, mostly centred in the pub or their homes.'

Lesbians begin socialising. Auckland's KG club had opened in 1969. *Pat O'Brien, Frances Mowatt.* The Karangahape Girls: a social club, a community, a place to be openly lesbian. *Esme Thompson, Kelly Newstubb, Lorraine Curel, Jill Hikuroa, Maureen Seagar, Judy Rose.* Lesbian weddings, *Shirley Tamihana* and *Jimmie.* But the original club closed in 1972. The lesbian feminists changed it all. The name went on to other venues, the pool table stayed the same. Now there are bars and clubs in downtown Auckland run as businesses, often shared with gay men. In Wellington, Club 41, raided by the police for breach of liquor laws, carried on. For a while.

In Christchurch in 1973, Sisters for Homophile Equality (SHE) forms. Gay women unite and work with the local women's movement. SHE starts the country's first women's refuge for battered women and children. (Later, lesbians in the refuge movement were to become a 'problem' for some straight women, making it not always easy for lesbians to work there.) Meeting and socialising. Separate from the gay men *and* working with gay brothers.

Coming out (saying 'I am a gay woman') at work, to family, in sports groups or anywhere is a punishable crime. Fathers dismiss the marching team's coach when she comes out. Others have their daughters psychoanalysed for being lesbian. Public education, public speaking, consciousness raising. *Gail, Anne, Chrissie, Sandy Hall, Jo Crowley, Susan, Allie. Morrigan Severs*: 'There were thirty of us.' *Marilyn*: 'There's much more than you have written.'

A few months later SHE Wellington publishes *Lesbian Feminist Circle* (*Circle*), initially with Christchurch SHE. 'It is our purpose to unite the lesbians of New Zealand as part of the ever growing international movement of gay women.' *Glenda, Alison, Viv, Ann, Gael, Porleen, Marilynn, Valda, Jill, Edel, Laurien, Dianne, Norma, Jan, Jenny* produce the first issue, December 1973, in one 16 hour day at *Alison*'s house. *Circle* will appear monthly for the first year, then quarterly, then irregularly, until 1985.

The 1973 United Women's Convention in Auckland has a homosexual women's workshop. Lesbians become increasingly visible at the conventions, until the fourth and last in Hamilton in 1979. Issue 10 of *Broadsheet*, June 1973, has lesbians on the cover and a lesbian article inside, both the work of *Sharon Alston*. 'I thought Sharon Alston was very brave as she was the only out lesbian I knew in 1971.'

I (the writer) am not there yet.

It is a time of questioning: violence in the social scene, alternatives to money, dreams, visions of the future. Passions. Sex, sexuality. Gay liberation. Women's liberation. Telling parents: hurt, anger—them and us. Jokes, cartoons, songs: getting together. Sexism. They say the only okay is heterosexual. Lesbians say women together (in every way, including sexually) is liberating. And wonderful. We dream of a future where we are. Laughing.

The first national lesbian conference is held in Wellington, March 1974, organised by *Jill Harvey* and *Marilynn Johnson. Sharon Alston, Alison Laurie, Jo Crowley, Allie, Rae Dellaca, Maureen Thompson, Robyn, Saj, Romi Curl, Lynne Paskaless, Jan Smith* were there. Who else? *Marilynn* ensured a women-only press—very radical for those days. Feminism and lesbianism: gay women are the women's movement. There's a lesbian in every woman.

There are papers on feminism and lesbianism, the international gay movement, lesbian mothers; workshops on what is a lesbian?, lesbian sexuality, lesbians in the workforce, lesbians and our families, lesbian mothers, and lesbians in the gay and women's movements. The women's movement is paranoid about lesbians. Spoiling the image?

1975, Herstory Press: *Robin Sievewright, Jill Hannah.* For the next five years they print women's work, including the first women's art magazine *Circle*, and bring in and sell lesbian-feminist books from overseas.

Sexual identity is an issue: transsexuals, transvestites. The boundaries of sisterhood are drawn. There is acknowledgement, support, limited political agreement. We are women—from birth.

The Auckland Women's Centre bars a lesbian who is in the police force. Feminists are suspicious of lesbians 'in the system'. For many it's better to be downwardly mobile and outside the system.

Meanwhile lesbians create relationships, friendships, lover-ships, invent sexuality. Go for quality, fail, try again. Lesbian-feminists are endlessly fascinated by the how-to of relationships. They challenge themselves and others to do it differently. *Heather*: 'Multiple relationships—our name for non-monogamy. It became the catchphrase for a philosophy of anti-patriarchal, non-possessive relating ... It led to clarity of purpose and approach rather than what many felt was the unacknowledged dishonesty and double standard of heterosexual relationships.' Monogamy is patriarchal rule. 'Finding one could be best friends with ex-lovers or be lovers with friends went against all learnt/taught theories of women's "competitiveness". Close but loose lesbian communities.'

Annual National Gay Liberation conferences. How productive

were they? How possible is working with gay men? Some get tired, disillusioned. Others continue. In Auckland, GALA (Gays and Lesbians on Air), Gay/Lesbian Welfare, The Isherwood Trust, ALGY (Auckland Lesbian and Gay Youth). In Christchurch, Crosses and Arrows, Gay/Lesbian Broadcast Collective, Lambda Centre. And in Wellington, the Gay and Lesbian Community Centre and LAGANZ (Lesbian and Gay Archives of New Zealand). Recent controversy over who (must they be openly lesbian and gay?) can make decisions about the archive has angered some lesbians.

The Gay Feminist Collective forms in Auckland in 1974: *Sharon Alston, Maureen Thompson, Jan Smith*, who else?

Women's issues are lesbian issues—rape, abortion, violence, equal pay, child care, incest. And then there are lesbian issues— prejudice in families, at work, on the streets. Invisibility. Self-hatred. Jobs lost. Training lost. Families lost. 'Cures' range from moral pressure to electroshock.

Lesbian mothers: lesbian right or heterosexual privilege? There's a regular section in *Circle* at the beginning. Some are mothers first—in time, that is. Some are lesbians first. To choose to be a mother or not. Boy children. Strong feelings. Lines drawn. Later, battles over custody, money, co-parenting, the rights and responsibilities of the non-biological mother when the relationship between the mothers ends. Family has different meanings to lesbians—it can include a community of friends, ex-lovers. This is particularly important to lesbians rejected by FOOs (Families Of Origin). Non-sexist child rearing. We are (mostly) the children of heterosexual parents. Our children, too, will develop their own sexuality. We don't *make* them anything, any more than our parents made us lesbian. But they might know of more options.

Debbie Jones defines heterosexism in *Broadsheet*: 'The system-atic enforcement of heterosexuality and corresponding attempt to eliminate homosexuality.' Marriage is a tool of the patriarchy. Lesbianism is a political statement: by being lesbian, lesbians demonstrate that there is an alternative to heterosexuality. Now *that's* threatening.

Making lesbians visible. Seven go to a straight ball in Wellington, have a ball (this is 1974). Lesbians think, write, talk about what's wrong with the world, how women are oppressed, exploited, abused. SHE publishes a manifesto.

The Crimes Amendment Bill (1974) reveals MPs' prejudices. Lesbians could become illegal in the same way as male homosexuals. Call to action: write to MPs (especially those on the select committee), make posters, stickers, go on talkback radio, send letters to editors, write articles. Fight against being made criminals. Lesbian mothers have special concerns. The (gay) Homosexual Law Reform Society doesn't listen to lesbians. On 4 July 1975 the Bill is lost in parliament by 34 votes to 29. Twenty-nine MPs think lesbianism should be criminalised.

Writing arrives from the North American Furies (Charlotte Bunch and others): Sexism is the root of all oppressions; lesbianism is the basic threat to male supremacy; lesbianism is a political choice.

Lesbians work in women's centres, rape crisis, women's refuge, *Broadsheet*, all across the women's movement. Women Against Pornography, *Ruth Charters, Trish Mullins*. Lesbians take part in gay pride week. Lesbians in all kinds of radical/change settings: unions, EEO, working on domestic violence among lesbians, in refuge, rape crisis, Women's Studies. Lesbian Studies. Lesbians write, think and talk about relationships. Lesbians read and review and talk about books: *The Descent of Woman, Our Bodies Ourselves, Rubyfruit Jungle, Patience* and *Sarah*. We tell and write personal stories, poems. Love poems. Hurt poems.

At a lesbian be-in at Waikato University, the question is asked, 'Why are you so aggressive about coming out?' The problem for lesbians is heterosexism. The Values party takes a stand on homosexuality—it's okay, well sort of, we might need to think about some things some more.

International news and contacts. *Alison Laurie* writes a poem, 'To A Danish Lesbian Friend Who Committed Suicide'. *The Girls' Guide* gives international travel information.

1975. Who is International Women's Year for? Not lesbians. Three minutes at the convention plenary session. Lesbian workshops open to heterosexual women. Some withdraw to a lesbian-only group. Others educate and face hostility. *Rosemary, Dianne, Jo*. And many dozen others. Were you there?

The tyranny of structurelessness meets Lesbian Nation. How can we run our groups to honour differences? How do we work together without destroying each other? North American Jill

164

Johnston lights the fires of controversy. 'All women are lesbians except those who don't know it ... until women see in each other the possibility of a primal commitment which includes sexual love they will be denying themselves the love and value they readily accord to men thus affirming their second class status.' Many lesbians love it, many other women are insulted.

Lesbians take action about rape, abortion. Women have a right to control their bodies. Every women's issue is a lesbian issue. Is every lesbian issue ... ? No.

Separatism. Sexuality. Relationships. The SCUM (Society for Cutting Up Men) manifesto and other heady writing from overseas. What the word lesbian means to us. *Heather*: 'Clearing our shelves of men's books, art, music so that women's voices could be heard—specifically local women. Becoming pragmatic and integrating sexuality/spirituality. Researching religion and realising "man-made" spirituality seriously limits women's realisation of their potentials.'

Separatism, alternative lifestyles apart from men and the patriarchy—psychically and/or physically. Some say separatism is the vanguard of feminism. Others say it won't change conditions for the majority of women. We focus attention on ourselves. The personal is political. We nurture and support each other. Is it a temporary tactic or a long-term strategy? A state of mind. Evolving revolutionary women unrestricted by men. It's an international movement. An unnamed correspondent: 'The strength of separatism has sustained lesbianism. Separatism hasn't been fairly dealt with; it's been dismissed as "cultural" feminism (and therefore, by implication, not "political") and trashed as "personal solution". Separatist lesbians have been aggressively attacked for being aggressive. Separatist lesbians are still active, not all are "names", many are involved and respected locally, living a life for and with lesbians.'

Passion. Politics. Coming out stories. And relationships, always relationships. Falling in love—again. What's left if you cut out romance? Monogamy, monotony. The woman in your life is you. Sex. Living together or not. Non-monogamy as relationships in transition. Laughter.

Amazon softball club, Wellington, 1977. Three years later Circe in Auckland. Soccer and softball. Playing each other and entering local competitions. For some, competitiveness spoils the spirit.

Finding our herstory: Sappho, Eleanor Roosevelt, Katherine Mansfield, Virginia Woolf, Doreen and Margaret (*Broadsheet*, November 1987) film stars, writers, ourselves, our mothers and grandmothers. *Morrigan* and other lesbians who work or have worked in women's refuge are gathering their stories.

At the 1977 United Women's Convention lesbians claim speaking time. *Linda Evans* makes a statement which is later printed in the conference book, *Changes, Chances, Choices*:

> I have been given time to speak to you today after a special request to the conveners. This is the first time there has been an opportunity for a lesbian to speak to a United Women's Convention about lesbian-feminism. I hope that at future conventions a lesbian speaker will be invited automatically.
>
> Many lesbians have worked long and hard in the feminist movement and it is time for open acknowledgement of our politics and our needs at gatherings such as this. We are no longer prepared to have our lesbianism written off as merely a matter of sexual preference. It hurts when other women accept men's definitions of us; those which define us purely on a sexual basis.
>
> We are women who have chosen to love other women, a commitment which involves our whole lives. We have seen that the oppression of women is organised and perpetuated by men and we have chosen to withdraw our energy from them. We are no longer dependent on male protection, approval or acceptance for our survival. We are defining our own identities.
>
> But to live such a life, a lesbian life, in man-made heterosexual society can be a perilous undertaking. To get some idea of what I mean by this, I suggest you go home from this convention and announce to your family that you are a lesbian. Walk along the street hand-in-hand with a woman friend. Kiss a woman in public. Tell your employer and workmates. But be prepared for hostility, withdrawal and ignorance.
>
> Over the weekend a woman asked me what went wrong with my childhood that I should be a lesbian now. I don't think that I am a deviant, someone who 'has been messed up'. And in speaking to you I am not asking for tolerance or sympathy for lesbians. I want to challenge the way you see yourselves, the limits you have accepted.

We are not separate from you. As a child, every woman's closest relationship was with another woman, her mother, and probably others. Yet how come after puberty we were all suddenly expected to devote our love and nurturing primarily to men?

Did you make that switch? How did it come about in your life? What were the pressures that forced you and the women around you to conform to the heterosexual pattern? Why were you forced to cut yourself off from the nurturing of other women in order to be emotionally and sexually exploited by men? Maybe this weekend you have begun to feel and imagine how things could be different. To see how women can communicate freely, hold each other, act together strongly, even make love with each other.

Many lesbians have decided to change society, not just cope with it. We have decided to do this by devoting our energies exclusively to developing women's strength, power and vision. We have been a motivating force in the women's movement and supplied much of its energy and leadership. We are part of any group active in issues affecting the ability of women to live autonomous lives independent of men, for example the abortion issue and the domestic purposes benefit—many lesbians are mothers.

It is because of lesbian activity that we finally have no men at this convention. We are by no means the only women who object to the intrusion of men. But we have been prepared, over the years, to consistently take action to remove them. WE are not the divisive element, THEY are.

Alongside these activities there is the joy, warmth and hope in the uncovering and strengthening of women's culture, some of which you may have participated in over the weekend. Living together, working together, lesbians brought you the Saturday night play, much of the music you have heard over the weekend, and organised the women's art show—all infused with woman-loving energy.

We're going to keep that energy going and we want you all there with us. We have hitherto been hindered in our communications with other women by a male media which, sensing our threat, distorts and trivialises our actions. Some of the coverage of this weekend has been just one example. We don't want to be separated from you again because we have at last had a chance of speaking to you directly.

And then the Piha Women's Liberation Conference, 1978. *Ripeka, Elizabeth, Jo Crowley, Donna, Rosemary, Dilys, Pilar, Morrigan, Jill.*

Over 100 women. For some it spelt the end of feminism as they knew it, or wanted it to be. Who calls lesbian feminism cultural feminism? Who calls cultural feminism lesser, not political? Who defines feminism? lesbianism? A split forms between lesbian and heterosexual feminists.

Broadsheet. A controversy over sharing rented space with a lesbian artists' group. A controversy over writing in *Broadsheet*. Some lesbians leave. *Romi, Rosemary, Val, Chris*. *Circle* withdraws support. Lines are drawn. Some cross over. Some don't.

Bronwen writes of 'how much less visible lesbians were in the early seventies. The only references to lesbians in my adolescence and twenties were in psychology books (deviance) and the odd court case like Parker and Hulme (deviance again). It was incredibly difficult to be out. The few lesbian community initiatives such as SHE (Christchurch), and *Circle* (Wellington) and *Broadsheet* collective members coming out publicly were incredibly brave for those times, but they were not happening on a big scale.'

The Women's Gallery (Wellington, 1980) and publishing collective Spiral grow with lesbian energy. *Heather*: 'Many lesbian artists opened up to art through the women's art movement which sought to demystify sources of art and re-site it in our lives and community—hence most lesbian homes have paintings/postcards/cards/books/hangings by local lesbian painters and poets and photographers and fabric artists.'

From 1983 Wellington has a weekly lesbian radio programme, with *Alison Laurie* and *Linda Evans* as its mainstays. Other programmes go to air in Christchurch, Auckland, Dunedin.

Names for lesbians, not all used now: lezzies, dykes, queers, slacks (from the forties), kamp girls, butch, femme, busdriver, friends of Dorothy.

The Lesbians Unite Fire Brigade write for *Circle* and raise issues of class in feminism. It's often lesbians who raise new issues. *Linda, Robyn, Jill, Hilary, Debbie*. I can't quote them here— *Circle* is restricted for women only.

Guardianship Amendment Bill. *Yoka Neuman* (in the name of the National Gay Rights Coalition) submits a clause saying there should be no presumption that homosexuality in a parent will adversely affect the welfare of a child. No chance of getting that in! Yoka starts the Lesbian Mothers' Defence Fund in Dunedin.

Circle prints the names of contact lesbians all around the country but the Lesbian Centre cannot put this advertisement on Wellington buses: 'Lesbians: Contact your local lesbian community. Write to [Box No], Wellington.' Lesbians may drive the buses but not advertise on them.

Witches, Bitches and Dykes, a women's liberation newspaper, begins in Auckland. Most who work on it are lesbians. Meanwhile *Circle* continues. *Porleen, Anne, Annie, Nina, Carol, Kathleen, Jean.* An emergency issue in November 1982 asks, What is *Circle* to be? A non-critical forum? No. Yes. More radical? More communication between feminist and non-feminist lesbians? Faster production? Who is to do it? The last *Circle* is produced by a group of lesbians in Manawatu: *Nicola, Chris, Linda, Sophie, Helena.* They don't know it will be the last.

Bronwen writes: 'The foreigners were tremendously important in early lesbian initiatives—German, English, American—often travelling around getting passed on to new households. Also important were those New Zealand women who had experienced lesbian alternative lifestyles in other countries. The Germans, particularly, influenced ideas in the South Island, many migrating in chains after meeting New Zealanders in Europe. These chains are still continuing today. The annual influx of athletic Americans en route to and from Antarctica from 1979 to the present have made a big impact on the Christchurch lesbian community and started international links that are still operating.'

But not everyone agrees about the importance of foreigners: 'The overseas women were stimulating and brought new ideas but were peripheral, not central to group intitiatives in my experience.'

In 1984 the first New Zealand book about lesbians, never mind lesbian mothers, is produced, *Amazon Mothers* by *Miriam Saphira*. It has local research, and information for social workers, other professionals and, of course, us. It is published by Papers Inc.—in other words *Miriam*, with help from friends.

Music. *The Women's Allstar Band, Vibraslaps, Dead Famous People, The Dolphins, Turiiya, Freudian Slips, Hilary King, Di Cadwallader, The Topp Twins, Jess Hawk Oakenstar, Meryl Yvonne, Debbie Filler, Mahinaarangi Tocker, Mereana Pitman.* Singing in pubs, at gatherings, concerts, conferences, in the street. The Topps block Queen St.

A Lesbian Support Group, begun in Auckland in 1980, is still going. *Jude Dean*. For years there was a regular weekly support group. Dozens of lesbians worked in it. *Dianne, Cherry, Jan.* Who else? Now there's an advertisement in the *Herald* and an answerphone. Facilitators are being trained to run regular coming out groups.

The Auckland Dyke Ball, the first Saturday in July, has been the annual fundraiser for the Lesbian Support Group since the early eighties. The first was a combined birthday/farewell party for two local lesbians, then *Jude* and others picked it up as a fundraiser. There's also been a Dyke Ball in Dunedin for the last couple of years, and one in Christchurch 1992.

In 1984 *Zoe Catherine Alice* writes *Waxing Moon, the Lesbian Herstory Archives*. In *Zoe*'s house—papers, articles, magazines, personal letters and journals, photographs, ephemera. Call for contributions. Now it's in boxes somewhere. No resources (money). No place. 'Where the hell can we put our archives?'

Lesbians have to deal with doctors. Do you tell her or him? Choose the doctor carefully. If you can—there may be only one in town. Then there's hospitals. They have got better and usually the partner you love can visit. What if you're too afraid to ask? You get to see your family, whom you may not be close to, more than your lover?

All lesbians are NOT equal. Class. Race. Racism. Maori lesbians. Lesbians of colour. Sisterhood is diverse. Some say, 'You oppress me with your language, your dress, your assumptions, your ignorance, white, middle-class lesbian.' If no one has any power maybe it will be okay. (Some chance.) Challenges. Guilt. Pain. Withdrawal. Re-grouping. Reading. Analysis. Talking. It's never going to be easy.

The press. *Paula Wallis* in *Broadsheet*, after studying some 1983 newspapers: 'We are considered newsworthy only when a news item is outrageous enough to consolidate current prejudice.' Mostly negative entries, about gay men.

Lesbian mothers hold a weekend at Swanson with partners and children. With child care and workshops on custody, hyperactivity, relationships, child support and coming out.

Lesbians are involved in protests against celebrating the signing of the Treaty of Waitangi in 1980 and the anti-Springbok tour movement in 1981. Lesbians take anti-racism sessions, challenge institutional racism, support Maori activists. And raise the issue of race in lesbian feminist groups.

Maori lesbians meet together, when they can. Maori and lesbian. Wahine mo nga Wahine o te Moana nui a Kiwa (Auckland). Groups form in Wellington and Christchurch.

Bronwen again: 'My impression of what most lesbians were doing from the late seventies and early eighties was searching for a community. This included finding each other and experimenting with different ways of living together, usually independently of the patriarchy.' Hag's Farm on Banks Peninsula (*Rye, Soren, Pagan, Jude, Liz, Gill, Tor*) and Takaka (started by *Deidre* and *Ky*). Others in Northland (Earthspirit, Lesbian Haven) and Coromandel. 'Summer camp in Christchurch was part of this movement, giving lesbians a brief look at how a lesbian nation might work. There were also the group houses in the cities, where new women coming to town could stay, make connections and contribute new ideas to the local community: Trafalgar St and later Ranfurly St in Christchurch, Wallace St in Auckland and Salamanca Rd in Wellington.' Summer camp started in 1975: sun, swimming, workshops. In 1992 and 1993, camps are held near Wellington.

1985. The year of the Homosexual Law Reform Bill campaign. Fran Wilde attempts to reform the law. Lesbians and gays vs the religious right. Rallies, meetings, concerts, parades, coalitions, HUG (Heterosexuals Unafraid of Gays). Lesbian visibility. A full-page advertisement in the *New Zealand Herald* and other daily papers, names of lesbians, gays and supporters. The Salvation Army goes into the streets and door to door, seeking signatures on a petition opposing the Homosexual Law Reform Bill. (*Yoka* in Dunedin goes to their citadel and challenges their door-to-door tactics.) Wellington—forums, meetings, planning strategies. Difficulties (everywhere) working with gay men: different analysis, different strategies. Everywhere mobilise, organise, act, lobby, take risks too many to name. The right is scared we'll win. We don't. The gay men do, some.

LIP (Lesbians in Print) Auckland arises out of early homosexual law reform action. It's a classy production. For lesbians only. The first issue is made by *Marianne Doczi, Lindy McIntyre, Liz*

Lovell—alcohol and drugs are an issue—*Smith, Bernie Sheehan.* Then *Romi Curl* and *Phil McLean.* The October/November issue is produced by Wahine mo nga Wahine o te moana Nui a Kiwa.

Auckland, November 1986, lesbians celebrate. A four day festival, alcohol and drug free. LADA (Lesbian Alcohol and Drug Action) sets up something not alcohol based. *Dee Gulliver, Fe Day, Jill, Miriam, Jenny Rankine, Ingrid Huygens, Julie Helean, Romi Curl, Tanya Cumberland.* Three hundred women come from all over the country for the workshops, open forums, live music, cheap vego food, videos, fun run, creche, dance, softball, games, bookstall, crafts, rituals, art exhibition. Phew! Light on politics for some. Alcohol and drugs are an issue. Lesbians in recovery. For a while there is a group in Auckland called Straight Dykes. An in-joke.

Wellington Lesbians Newsletter number one, February 1988: activities, issues, a forum for discussion, sometimes heated, sometimes very heated. Started by *Jill Hannah, Marg Laird, Linda Evans.* Others do it now. It's restricted for lesbians only. Some of you reading these words will not understand this (or perhaps any other) lesbian separatist claim—for space, a newsletter, a gathering, a place to live that is for lesbians only. You will wonder why we do not want to (always) make ourselves available, if only to educate you. Well, you see, we have a drive to concern ourselves with ourselves. And that's the point—or one of them: to focus our attention on ourselves, not you.

National gay and lesbian weekend at Auckland's Carrington Polytechnic, Easter 1989. *Ngahui Te Awekotuku* delivers a speech 'Dykes and Queers', which is later published as an article in *Broadsheet,* and her collection of writings *Mana Wahine.* Lesbians caucus on bisexuality.

Wellington Lesbian Weekend, October 1989. Workshops on mental health, sex and sexuality, coming out, lesbian feminist politics, lesbians at work. Organisers: *Sheryl, Karen, Glenda, Nina, Jane, Porleen, Marg.* Over 40 other lesbians attend.

The press again, this time 1989. *Jenny Rankine* finds they keep us invisible, exclude us from 'the family', describe us like criminals, and link us with child abuse, while giving space to bigotry against us. AIDS means homosexuality gets more attention while lesbians continue to be invisible or misrepresented.

AIDS. Lesbians work with people with AIDS and develop safe

sex guidelines for lesbians. (Woman to woman transmission of HIV is not established.) Lesbians become HIV positive, mainly through drug needles.

When a lesbian is dying, is there room for her friends? *Gloria.* Everyone assumes the family will be in control—even if they haven't been close. Many lesbians know how to make wills, protect their lovers, make sure there's room for them and their friends when they die. Many don't.

Young lesbians form ALGY (Auckland Lesbian and Gay Youth) for support. *Rhiannon.* Getting into schools to speak to pupils. ALGY members successfully apply to the Lottery Board for funding for their work. Oh no! National MP Graeme Lee can't bear it. Quashes it.

Lesbian teachers. In these backlash days I don't want to name any. They meet together—quietly, of course. Lesbian nurses. They'd better be nameless too. Lesbian social workers. Shhhh. Lesbian any and everythings: accountants, carpenters, real estate agents, cleaners, unemployed, union organisers. Don't say she's a lesbian, it may cost her her job, or promotion. Yet some can be who they are everywhere they are, even at work. It depends.

Lesbian artists: some name themselves loudly, some softly, some not at all. Some want to be named only in lesbian places. *Sally Smith,* who co-curated Queer Pictures at the time of the Homosexual Law Reform Bill. *Lauren Lethal, Mary Moon, Willow, Carol Stewart, Fran Marno.* The artists in the new *Lesbian Spiral,* and in Gay and Lesbian Art curated by Marian Evans in Dunedin, 1992.

From 1990 New Zealand's immigration laws allow lesbians and gays to gain residence here for partners from overseas. They have to have evidence of a relationship that is 'genuine, stable and of at least four years' duration'. For heterosexuals a two year relationship will do.

Where now?

Lesbian newsletters, always. Lesbians love newsletters. And in the absence of geographically-based communities ('What about Grey Lynn?' says a voice behind my shoulder) we need them for contact. *Lesbian Links* in Nelson, *Tamaki Makaurau Lesbian Newsletter, Wellington Lesbians Newsletter,* Christchurch's *Out Of Line,* started in 1988 in Christchurch by 'a few of us' who 'got together and decided it was time lesbian women in Christchurch organised a better way to keep in contact with one another'. Radio programmes on access radio—Wellington's, and Dunedin's *Talk Lesbian* begun in October 1991 by *Kate Winstanley. Paula, Monique, Jennifer, Su, Marg, Sandie* and *Janet* work on it too.

Then there are the books. Poetry. *Heather McPherson* and *Miriam Saphira* each read from their new books at the Women's Bookshop in Auckland as I am working on this essay. Stories. *The Power and the Glory and other Lesbian Stories* from Paper Inc. *Exploding Frangipani* and *New Women's Fiction.* Ngahuia Te Awekotuku's *Tahuri* and *Mana Wahine Maori.* Novels, many published by New Women's Press. *Frances Cherry's Dancing With Strings. Renee's Willy Nilly.* Truth. *Julie Glamuzina* and *Alison Laurie's Parker and Hulme: A Lesbian View. Miriam* writes to me: 'All that energy, all that talent and yet we have so little currently in print by New Zealand lesbians.'

Contacts, networks, it's all fairly individual just now. The Lesbian Nationa-al Network from Wellington. The Older Lesbians Network from Christchurch. POLLY (Proud Older Lesbians Like You) starts, fades, revives in Auckland: a newsletter and regular getting together for talk, food, cards, outings, laughter. I hear there's one starting in Hamilton. Lesbians caucus at Women's Studies conferences. And wasn't it at the Feminist Educators' Conference in Christchurch in 1990 that the lesbian caucus passed a resolution that 25 December be declared National Lesbian Day and a public holiday, and didn't the whole conference endorse the resolution?

More lesbians are becoming mothers, on purpose.

Some current debates: sexual 'freedom' versus censorship and 'safety' (not a hot topic here yet, wait); feminist definitions and uses of power (a personal interest elevated to a debate?); how to be 'political' in a time of far right economics; individualism and community; inventing our relationships with each other; survival—ours, as individuals and communities, and the planet's; poverty.

It's hard to find a movement just now. Some lesbians are meeting political ambitions through involvement in straight organisations such as unions. Some are venturing into the more formal political arena. There's Gay-Lesbian Welfare, the Isherwood Trust, the Gay Business Association, Coming Out groups. Pamphlets are being produced on lesbians and the law, and ethical concerns for lesbians being counselled by lesbians. We teach each other line dancing. And we talk, sing, play and laugh together.

I have not resolved the naming dilemma. There are not enough lesbians named here. Not enough to demonstrate the wealth and depth of lesbian living: a trickle, not the full, flowing river that is our recent past.

Survival among the outcrops and troughs of the level playing field of contemporary New Zealand life is success. Too much personal solution and not enough politics, some say. I think we're learning to be kinder to each other, politically and personally, and that's not a bad thing. We have learnt about classism, racism, disability, and know enough not to pretend they aren't there. We agonise and try. (It is so maddening to be around men who are 'trying'. It must be as frustrating for Maori lesbians, lesbians of colour, lesbians with disabilities, to be around us).

Class, with its fuzzy definitions, remains something of an invisible issue. And all women's issues are still lesbian issues. Old issues like rape and violence, equity at work, and sexism don't go away. We add the new ones like understanding international economics, electoral reform, and privatisation of public services. Lesbian issues are still lesbian issues: heterosexism and homophobia still rule. And it's not okay.

Marilynn, you are right. We do have a feeling of strength for the future, 'in ourselves and in relation to the world'. Our pride and power as lesbians. Our working to 'evolve a consciousness that is life-generating and female-centred'. Our relationships with our lovers, friends, ex-lovers, ex-lovers' children, parents, siblings, Aunt Toni Cobbley and all. We create new (today they are new, really they are very old) social and emotional ways of being. As you say, *Marilynn*, we are 'a dazzle of sparkling lights'.

Acknowledgements

Responsibility for everything that is written here (or missing) is totally mine. My thanks to the following, for additions, comments and insights: Pilar Alba, Jo Crowley, Romi Curl, Fe Day, Bronwen Dean, Linda Evans, Julie Glamuzina, Marilynn Johnson, Debbie Jones, Glenda Laurence, Heather McPherson, Jenny Rankine, Lisa Sabbage, Miriam Saphira, Morrigan Severs.

175

Hairy Questions

CHARMAINE POUNTNEY

YOU ASK ME ABOUT THE NEXT generation of women: What are they like? What are their values? Where are they headed? I wish I could give you a straight answer.

As guest speaker at a leadership course at a girls' school, I find none of the issues I raise with these articulate fourth formers prompts as much response as a casual remark about women with hairy legs.

With a group of young Maori women planning tribal education developments, I find they talk with insight about the roots of their oppression in colonisation—land seizures, economic exclusion, rape of land and waterways, and contempt for Maori language in schools and the media—but not about 'women's issues'.

Discussing the possibility of genuine partnership relationships with a group of sixth and seventh formers at an expensive private school, I notice the talk is dominated by half a dozen students (three boys, three girls; five Pakeha, one Chinese) who express hostile attitudes and little understanding of Maori issues of land, culture and language. No one wants to talk about gender at all.

What conclusions can be drawn from such experiences? That body image—to shave or not to shave, to diet or not to diet—is the most pressing concern of many young articulate Pakeha women? That many Maori women have no time or energy to confront sexism when faced every day with far grosser imbalances between Maori and Pakeha? That many private school students are racist and ignorant and have little interest in gender equality? Since systematic research on the relative situation of women and men over the last 20 years in this country is scarce, I have to make do with such snippets of evidence and with my own experience in educational institutions.

In 1978 I was appointed headmistress of Auckland Girls' Grammar School. It's clear to me now that had I been a radical feminist then I would never have been considered for the job. As my feminist beliefs developed during my decade at Auckland Girls' Grammar, I became increasingly uneasy. When I made even the most mild comments in public, abusive phone calls and anonymous letters arrived from around the country. On one such occasion all I had done was reflect on why the media gave such prominence to rugby when netball was much more pleasurable to watch—this was in the early eighties, before Television New Zealand had discovered the Silver Ferns (New Zealand's world-class women's netball team). During 1979 and 1980 some parents accused me of rampant feminism. Others removed their daughters from the school because of what they called 'undesirable feminist influences'. The irony was that at this stage most of us on the staff had not developed even a rudimentary feminist analysis.

Later in the eighties when we had, I was frequently asked to speak out on public issues. I was torn. I knew that to speak out was to risk alienating the large number of conservative students and their families in the school. That would have meant a loss of pupils, a falling roll, fewer staff and fewer opportunities for the remaining students—those whose parents couldn't afford to sent them elsewhere. And there were personal risks. If I had expressed my deeply held convictions on homosexuality, the fashion industry, the Miss New Zealand contest, abortion and Maori sovereignty, I have no doubt I would have been asked to resign, or been sacked.

It was the classic feminist dilemma. Should I remain moderate and careful in public to ensure the survival of Auckland Girls' Grammar School as a relatively benign and strengthening environment for young women? Or should I risk censure for myself and the school by trying to raise public consciousness? The school, as a strong female institution, was in itself a challenge to patriarchal society. A public dispute would probably have damaged it. Some parents and school board members had already sought to have me removed. And my resignation in such circumstances would certainly have ensured the appointment of a more conservative successor.

Later, my experiences as principal of Hamilton Teachers' College and then as principal and dean of the University of Waikato School of Education were to make me wary of the reactions of politicians. The new tertiary funding regime had given the Minister of Education the power to decide which institutions received funding for which programmes, regardless of the advice given by the Ministry of Education. Over the years the paranoid reactions of male MPs on both sides of the House have given me little confidence in politicians' objectivity or intelligence. Had I gone public with my criticisms of government policy and practice, funding for teacher education places in Hamilton could well have been cut. Just as in 1990 the newly elected National government cut the funding for the University of Waikato Law School, headed by feminist and former Labour party president Margaret Wilson, the only other female dean of a university professional school.

My experience in education has taught me that women are acceptable in leadership positions only as long as they behave in ways which do not seriously threaten the social order set up and controlled by men—the very order feminism seeks to undo. In theory I should have felt bolder and more powerful as I moved up the educational ladder, but the opposite was the case.

Even in the nineties our education system is still a patriarchal pyramid. Tens of thousands of poorly paid or unpaid women (and a few men) care for and educate children at the bottom, and a few hundred highly paid male academics, bureaucrats, principals and politicians (and a few women) control the systems at the top, and maintain the status quo with all their might. Being a minority, women in elevated positions often feel isolated and alienated. For me, moving from the supportive, egalitarian staff relationships at Auckland Girls' Grammar, where all of the senior staff and most of the other staff were women, to male-dominated secondary school principals' meetings, and later to teachers' colleges and universities, was not a pleasant experience.

Principals' meetings, like those of academic boards and councils, are almost always masculine in style. For women used to the more rational, warm, quick-thinking, task-centred and playful behaviour of women's groups, trying to operate in them is exasperating and abrasive. Trying to challenge or change them is self-defeating. In the end, male power is usually further entrenched and would-be change agents well and truly marginalised.

In the late eighties I watched with morbid fascination the way a group of sexist, racist and homophobic Auckland secondary principals formed a coalition to exclude those they perceived as threatening. They co-opted acquiescent Maori and female principals and set up new local and national power structures led by mediocre men. This was the origin of the Secondary School Principals' Association of New Zealand, established to oppose changes being promoted by the New Zealand Post-Primary Teachers' Association.

It's easy to see this process as malicious, but I am inclined to a more generous interpretation. As a Pakeha who in recent years has been challenged to face up to my own prejudice and to the structural racism in our society, I have learned that most discrimination comes from inertia, ignorance, foolishness and fear.

This doesn't make change any easier. And yet if I look back to my own schooling in the fifties, and to conditions in schools when I started teaching in the sixties, I realise there has been change and that much of it has come about through feminism.

In 1953 when I attended Cornwall Park School, girls were not allowed to be school patrols. No reasons were given, it was an unarguable policy. It was also unarguable that girls must do cooking and boys woodwork. Never mind that I could already cook meals, bake cakes and bottle fruit, but couldn't tell a hacksaw from a handsaw. In 1954 at the brand new Remuera Intermediate School, I was again consigned to the resented and unnecessary cooking and sewing classes while the boys did exciting (in my eyes anyway) things with wood and metal. As a girl, I was not allowed to sit the Rawlings Scholarship examination, even though I was better at schoolwork than any of my male classmates, and just as competitive. It's not surprising that by the end of the year I was having fantasies of dressing in boys' uniform to break into the forbidden world of male opportunity. I rued the short and chubby body which would have made such a disguise impossible.

Not all schools have changed. Only a few years ago I interviewed a young woman for enrolment at Auckland Girls' Grammar. She and her mother were still fighting for her right to learn the full range of technicraft skills and share equally with boys in the rights and responsibilities of her West Auckland primary school. By then it was a rare primary or intermediate school which discriminated against girls so crassly and obviously, but the battle for equal treatment is far from won.

Too many girls entering secondary school still have horror stories to tell about sexist language and behaviour in their primary and intermediate schools. Between 1978 and 1988 I interviewed a couple of hundred 12-year-olds a year, from more than 60 different schools. Many wanted to come to a girls' school because of irritation at having their work disrupted by immature, aggressive boys, and the tendency of teachers to pander to male students and perpetuate sexist stereotypes.

Boys' continuing aggression—verbal and physical—in our primary schools has been documented by Karen Newton and Lise Bird. In 'John says a few words, Margaret listens', published in *Women and Education in Aotearoa II*, Newton reported that 69 percent of verbal interactions between teacher and pupil during morning talks were with boys. In 'Girls taking positions of authority in primary schools', Bird described how even in classrooms where equality was consciously encouraged, and girls given a fair share of leadership roles and responsibilities, boys behaved more violently outside class time than their female classmates.

From the late seventies feminists tried to change this. Feminist teachers and their colleagues in universities carried out research, raised the awareness of parents and teachers, and promoted practical ways of bringing about change. In pre-service training primary teachers can now study equity issues and how they affect classroom behaviour. Female principals and middle management (and the occasional male teacher and board of trustees member) have flocked to leadership courses drawing on local feminist and international research. In 1989 the government education reform package Tomorrow's Schools gave strong support to equity principles. Many schools wrote charters with clear anti-racism and anti-sexism clauses—and retained them even after Minister of Education Lockwood Smith removed the legal requirement in 1991.

However, the proportion of parents and primary teachers who really support and practise anti-sexist education is probably still less than 10 percent. Although even this would be a huge increase on the number who 30 years ago even realised there was a problem.

And what of our secondary schools? Like most girls of my generation I went to a single sex secondary school. There were no men on the staff of Epsom Girls' Grammar except the caretaker. Women and girls ran everything—from film projectors, field trips and physics labs to swimming, Scottish country dancing, debating, drama and discus throwing. We were monitors, patrols, technicians, house captains and prefects. Our uniforms were quaintly sedate. From time to time prefects' patrols checked hats, gloves and stockings. Other than that, no one made much of a fuss about clothes. We sensed instinctively that uniform checks were more about maintaining discipline and control than about whether our dress was appropriate. Fashions were not much discussed, at least among my friends. Neither were boys, except around the time of the Grammar Ball when we suddenly had to acquire one as a partner. Nobody I knew ever talked about diets or agonised over their thighs. It was assumed that most of us in the academic stream would go on to university. We were encouraged to do mathematics and science, although only one fifth form and one sixth form class out of eight did a full science course. At no stage during my five years at Epsom was I aware of obstacles to academic opportunities.

It's easy now to look back and see what was missing. There was no preparation for our roles as adult women, partners or mothers. No one told us there could be a conflict between what we wanted to do and what society expected us to do. Most of our teachers were single women who had been teachers all their adult lives. Married women were seldom promoted to responsible positions. Our role models of women in charge were single and childless. The only vocational guidance I remember was a mass talk in the fifth form which suggested nursing, teaching or secretarial work. Those were our options. No one mentioned politics, archaeology or engineering. Law (which is what I should probably have studied) didn't get a look in. One teacher urged some of us to become research scientists. A student from the upper sixth was going to train as a doctor, encouraged by her school inspector father. We were dimly aware that women could be librarians. But that was as far as it went. Bright students, usually from well off families, were cocooned by the system of streaming which was almost universal. Those of us in the upper streams had little idea about the lives of other students. We had sparse or no contact with Maori students, working class students or indeed anyone significantly different from ourselves.

When I trained as a teacher in 1964 most secondary schools were still like this. So was Auckland Girls' Grammar School when I began work there in 1978. So were some South Island girls' schools I visited in 1987. To know this is to understand how dramatic the impact of teachers with feminist awareness has been. By the nineties most secondary schools had changed significantly. In all but a few, the most rigid limitations of subject choice and student grouping had been modified.

Although many teachers haven't changed, the systems that surround them have. Today's Quest Rapuara, for example, bears little resemblance to the Vocational Guidance Service which so successfully limited our horizons in the sixties. It produces good non-sexist materials and encourages students to look at a wide array of work and study options.

Until the squeeze on discretionary staffing in 1990 and 1991, secondary schools were also offering a wide range of personal support for young people. My experience at Auckland Girls' Grammar showed me that young people could be helped to deal effectively with some of the most hideous forms of physical, emotional and sexual abuse if there was a network of trusted peers and staff with time to nurture and empower students. The development of strong guidance networks—both within schools and with outside agencies—has been one of the most successful educational changes of the last generation.

Although the destructive effects of streaming on both students and teachers have, even now, never been fully acknowledged, in the seventies we at last started to challenge the boys-to-metalwork, girls-to-sewing mindset which had been entrenched in our schools since the thirties. The old divisions of academic, general and technical/commercial have gradually melted down into the flexible option systems now common to most secondary schools.

Gender-based assumptions about who should do what have proved more tenacious. Few girls take senior mathematics, computing, physics, chemistry and technology. Few boys opt for languages, art, music and history. Women activists in science and mathematics education have striven to change girls' perceptions of these subjects, and to transform the ways they are taught, but only a few male science and maths teachers have changed their ways. Few men at the top have come out and said we need to change boys' perceptions of subject choices, vocations, or anything much else. Even fewer have done anything about it.

Conservatism still prevails in many areas. Although most schools now have more flexible dress codes for senior students, very few have done away with uniforms. The vast majority of New Zealand teenagers are still forced to wear clothes which strive, against the odds, to make 15-year-olds look like five-year-olds, and which reinforce outdated sex stereotypes. This may not seem to be seriously related to issues of gender equity, but I believe that all aspects of schooling which are about ruling rather than learning help determine the power relationships in our society. Those schools which place the greatest emphasis on externally imposed discipline, childish uniforms and competitive success are the schools which are preparing young people to be rulers and ruled rather than partners and participants.

'Grice has spent his time reading,' Doris Lessing wrote in *The Sentimental Agents*, 'His prior education was largely designed to equip him for ruling, particularly to inculcate the conviction of superiority that in one way or another the administrators of Empire must have. He had no idea at all of the richness of information available about his own species.' Many schools are still producing Grices, still largely excluding the richness of information. This is not entirely their fault: much of the blame can be laid on a national examination system which tests irrelevant knowledge at the expense of a broader curriculum.

But the grossest example of ruling in schooling, corporal

punishment, was finally banned by law in 1987 after years of pressure from feminist women and supportive men in the Labour party. With the exception of a handful of so-called Christian institutions, our schools no longer daily reinforce the idea that it's acceptable for big people to hit smaller people. All the same, as long as punishment of some kind—whether by detention, suspension or humiliation—remains the primary method of control within schools, we should not be surprised if violence is perpetuated by the next generation.

The alternative is to teach people to understand themselves and others, and to behave in more considerate and self-controlled ways. Lamentably, such skills seldom figure in the curriculum. Only in schools where teachers consciously incorporate them into subjects such as English, Maori, health or social studies do they happen at all.

It's fair to say that in the sixties and seventies most improvements in education came about through teachers responding to students' needs, rather than from specifically feminist concerns. We were not revolutionaries. Before the 1979 United Women's Convention in Hamilton most of us had precious little understanding of sexism, heterosexism and racism. We didn't even know the words. The earlier women's conventions in 1973, 1975 and 1977 had concentrated on obvious flaws in the education system, such as restrictions on subject choices for girls, stifling examinations, hopeless vocational guidance, lack of child care facilities for staff, and the small number of women promoted to senior positions.

A new journey began for many of us that Easter in Hamilton. We were challenged to confront racism, heterosexism and homophobia in the women's movement and in New Zealand society. At the workshop I convened, my conservative critique of secondary education, which had changed little since I had started teaching, was rubbished by women with a clearer understanding of racism and sexism. Auckland Feminist Teachers and similar groups in other parts of the country were established as a result of the convention, and a more informed and organised feminist critique emerged through teachers' unions.

Eighty to 100 women crammed into some of the early Auckland Feminist Teachers meetings. They came from schools, universities and polytechnics, and the then Department of Education. Newsletters reached even greater numbers. For the first time there was a network of common concern and action among women in education, linking hundreds of us around the country. This wave of feminist action had significant results.

The New Zealand Post-Primary Teachers' Association had set up a committee on sex equality in 1976, but it was only after the emergence of Feminist Teachers that things started to happen. In 1981, after fierce debate, the PPTA adopted the United Nations Working Women's Charter. Four years later its first ever women's conference led to the establishment of an official network of women's representatives and the appointment of a women's advisory officer at its head office. A further women's conference in Dunedin in 1987 called for a national non-sexist resource centre to be set up. A special issue of the PPTA Journal in 1989 noted the establishment of the first women's studies course in a secondary school, research on girls in science and mathematics, changing management styles, and more women working in the union and in management positions in schools.

Meanwhile government machinery was slowly moving forward. In 1985 the Department of Education produced a resource pack on women in technical institutes. Three years later we finally saw the 'National Policy for the Education of Girls and Women in New Zealand'.

Just as important was a flowering of local feminist research, such as Ruth Fry's *It's Different for Daughters,* Margaret Wilson's groundbreaking *Report on the Status of Academic Women in New Zealand,* and Mollie Neville's *Promoting Women.* Sue Middleton of the University of Waikato compiled a rich collection of new research papers into *Women and Education in Aotearoa*—so popular it was followed in 1992 by *Women and Education in Aotearoa II,* edited by Middleton and Alison Jones of the University of Auckland.

Much of the research is depressing. But without it there would be little change. In 1983 Alison Jones approached Auckland Girls' Grammar to seek our co-operation in a research project. Its aim was to see whether, in a single sex school, race and social class might produce discrimination in the same way as gender did in coeducational schools. We were horrified when she fed back to us her observations of the unconsciously racist behaviour of staff, and the methods the girls themselves used to limit what they were taught. Thanks to the research we were able to change classroom practices in ways which had immediate and obvious benefits to the students.

Fragments, shreds of experience, dots and dashes of progress. Where are we going? Throughout the school system, girls are achieving better results than boys. More are staying on in secondary schools. More are going on to universities and polytechnics. More are studying law and medicine. But what of the teaching methods, the curricula, the structures? Is it different for daughters?

Alton-Lee questions whether encouraging girls to be successful within sexist curricula and school structures—the thrust of the last two decades—is either good for them at the time, or useful to them in the long-term:

> Traditionally, researchers have focused on inequalities of opportunity and achievement, and many strategies for change have been directed towards increasing girls' participation and achievement in male-dominated disciplines such as mathematics and science. Although there have been significant barriers to girls' achievement, such a focus can be misleading. On average, girls frequently do better and their achievement is seen as evidence that the education system is serving girls well . . .
>
> We argue that their achievements in a curriculum that undervalues and derogates women is deeply problematic for girls . . . that the curriculum is critical to the process by which many girls come to accept the subordination and invisibility of women.

She might have added that the problematic curriculum is matched by the problematic imbalance in teaching staff. Two decades after second wave feminism struck our shores, there is still no area in our education system where female and male teachers have equal status. The younger the children, the less likely they are to be taught by men, who make up a mere one percent of kindergarten teachers and 24 percent of primary teachers. Since many children see little of their fathers from day to day, young boys often have little experience of men in nurturing and educative roles. Nor will this change overnight: the proportion of men training for early childhood and primary teaching has not altered significantly in 10 years. At the top of the pyramid the position is just the reverse. Only three percent of women teaching in primary schools are principals, compared with 31 percent of men. In secondary schools, 0.4 percent of female teachers are principals and 29 percent are in positions of responsibility. For men the comparable figures are 3.6 and 46 percent.

Even this, though, is startling progress. When I started school, and later when I became a teacher, nearly all primary schools had male principals. All boys' and coeducational secondary schools were headed by men. It was the mid seventies before the first woman was appointed head of a coeducational secondary school—and by then several men had been appointed principals of girls' schools.

Feminist teachers and crusaders such as the PPTA's women's officer Helen Watson saw their efforts rewarded by a slight increase in the number of women in top positions—25 percent of primary school principals (8 percent in 1981) and 17 percent of secondary principals (11 percent in 1981). By 1990 three of the country's polytechnics, one College of Education, the Ministry of Education, and the Education Review Office were all headed by women.

Feminism's philosophic objection to individualistic, hierarchical leadership and its quest for alternatives have, for all this, failed to transform the New Zealand education world. Some schools (mostly with female principals, such as Karen Sewell at Green Bay High School, Edna Tait at Tikipunga High School and Ros Heinz at Hagley High School) have developed strong participatory management styles. However only two institutions have seriously challenged the male structural model. At Auckland's Selwyn College the board of trustees has appointed a woman and man as joint principals, and the new School of Education at Waikato University began with an executive group with parallel Maori and Pakeha leadership, and involved both men and women in top positions.

Much of the progress that has been noted here has been progress for Pakeha women. Maori are still being shortchanged— in pre-schools almost 40 percent of children are Maori but only 12 percent of teachers and child care workers; in primary schools the figure rises to 16 percent. This, though, is an improvement on a decade ago when the figures were 2 percent and 5 percent.

Although girls are now better educated than they used to be

in the old no-go subjects of mathematics, science and technology, boys have made little progress in their weak area—language. Boys make up the vast majority of poor listeners, readers and writers in our schools. Their spoken language is often confined to monologue, attempts to dominate the group or class, and aggressive debate. Most boys show little capacity for reflective, exploratory dialogue and the language of co-operative problem-solving. This is not surprising, as these kinds of language are seldom modelled for them by adult men. Nor are they rewarded in our competitive, sport-obsessed society. The fact that they are essential to the creative teamwork upon which modern inno-vation—not to mention good human relationships—depend seems to escape those responsible.

And who is responsible? Only men can provide appropriate role models for boys. Why aren't more men becoming teachers? Why aren't male politicians and businessmen promoting teaching as a career for men? Why aren't they giving more support and encouragement to fathers who share fully in parenting? Why aren't male organisations like Lions and Rotary tackling the prob-lem? Do they accept there is a problem? I personally can vouch for the fact they have been told.

But we must also remember that education does not happen only in educational institutions. The most powerful educative tool in our society is not the classroom but the television set. Young women—and young men—are daily conditioned and controlled by advertising copywriters, editors, film producers, programme controllers, priests and politicians, most of whom are male, middle-aged and mightily pleased with their own status and success. Anorexia, bulimia and a general obsession with body shape, diet, exercise, fashion, make-up and sexuality are far more common now than they were a generation ago, and insidious in their effects. And if the media work assiduously to push girls into strait-jacket stereotypes, they also deliver powerful punches to the brains of boys. Male violence, the major obstacle to a genuine partnership culture between women and men, is constantly boosted in the mass media's style of reporting sport, industrial relations and politics, and their obsession with crime and war.

At Auckland Girls' Grammar School, I was directly involved in the lives of hundreds of very different women and girls. I was forced to feel something of the pain and anger which sexism, heterosexism and racism cause in women's lives. The extent of the abuse of women in our society became apparent to all of us on the staff and we moved, through much reading and debate, towards some understanding of both the causes of oppression and the conditions needed for young people to develop their full potential. We were able to develop a community which was loving and empowering of young women and their families. We learned about the enrichment and delight of a diverse community which celebrates its differences. But we couldn't change the external forces which control power and resources. That requires a dramatically new coalition at a community level among those groups which have been savaged by the system—women, Maori, the unemployed—and those within the system who are willing and able to share their power.

Still, I am hopeful. A large number of young women emerging from the education system today are far more compassionate, articulate, well-informed and committed to personal and social change than my generation was. They have a clear feminist and anti-racist world view, and some are even unafraid of being lesbian. They are capable of shaping a better world—a new, decentralised and more co-operative society.

The rest, the majority, seem to me much like their mothers. Like their mothers, they will be altered by experience, age and, in subtle ways, by the voices and actions, pain and triumphs of their feminist sisters. Just as we were.

Unfinished Business

ANNE ELSE & ROSSLYN NOONAN

HELENA HUGHES

DAVID GURR

THROUGHOUT 1992, ROS AND I HAVE TALKED OFF AND on about what, if anything, our 20 years of active feminism have achieved. We have tried to make some sense of those years, to give ourselves—albeit very tentatively—some perspective on them. This essay is the result.

I first met Ros in 1960, when she arrived from Africa—where she had lived for 10 years with her journalist parents—to join the fifth form at Auckland Girls' Grammar School. Sandra Coney, Camille Guy and Susan St John were in the same class. We both married young, though we managed to complete degrees before we started having children (in my case, only just). I remember trying to tell one of my English professors how I felt about being at home with a baby, after the freedom of being a full-time university student. I couldn't say what I meant, and he couldn't hear me: 'It's just your *role* for a few years,' he said in a faintly exasperated tone.

In 1971, juggling jobs and child care, we each read Germaine

Greer's *The Female Eunuch*; I came down to visit Ros in Wellington and we talked about what was then called 'women's liberation' far into the night.

In those exhilarating early days of the women's liberation movement, we were certain women could do anything worth doing that men could do—but we would do it differently, so the world would be a better place for everyone. A characteristic New Zealand blend, perhaps, of the utopian, optimistic and naive—but it was a powerful conviction, fuelling a ferment of discussion, debate, activity and organisation.

The seventies saw an upsurge of women working together, discovering each other and our ability to organise, influence and change. We discovered the strengths and stresses of belonging to a group, and the joys and dilemmas of collective action. We were intoxicated with the developing insights and understandings that enabled us to begin to name the world and our own experiences, instead of men always naming it for us—from the doctors who were convinced that women knew nothing about how their own bodies worked, to the professors who taught entire history courses without mentioning a single woman.

We were rejecting the structures and stereotypes that divided us from each other, isolating us in our families and suburbs, and insisting that our identities and interests were established by and through men, and had to come perpetually second to theirs. We were tantalised by the prospect of a world where we could control our own lives. And we were convinced that with commitment and organisation, that goal was within our grasp.

Women met in formal consciousness raising groups and over cups of tea in each other's kitchens, at protest letter-writing sessions and public demonstrations, at small local group meetings and huge United Women's Conventions, at the early Women's Studies courses and the first workplace gatherings. Out of all the debate and discussion we sorted out the basics of what we wanted.

Women, we agreed, should be able to take as full a part in society as men, especially in political life. All the work we did for free—running households, having and bringing up kids, taking care of everyone who needed us—should be recognised for what it was: work, absolutely essential, skilled work. Women should be helped and supported to do their share of it—and so should men. We wanted good child care—for our sakes and our kids' sakes—and we believed early childhood services, like schools, should be funded through our taxes. We wanted fully equal pay, and an end to the antiquated systems and attitudes which kept down the pay for 'women's work', stopped most of us getting beyond the first rungs of the career ladders, and placed hundreds of jobs, from firefighter to managing director, out of bounds to any woman. We wanted every field of learning and training to be open to us. We wanted to take control of our own fertility and our own health issues, and to have our sexuality accepted. And we wanted society as a whole to take serious, public notice and effective action on every kind of violence against women. We succeeded in placing all these issues on the nation's political and social agenda—and made real progress on many of them.

Where did we come from? Compared with similar countries, sixties New Zealand had very few women in paid employment. Jobs were strictly divided along gender lines. A tiny number of women held prestigious or powerful positions—despite girls' relatively equal access to education. Sex education was banned from the classroom. Contraception was carefully fenced off from the single, and even from some of the married. Getting an abortion was a nightmare, and rates of births to single women, especially teenagers, were among the highest in the Western world. Domestic and sexual violence was (and still is) widespread. Many New Zealand women thought they had a good marriage if their men gave them enough money to manage on, didn't get drunk more than once a week, didn't take what the women earned (including the family benefit), and didn't beat them up. On top of all this, every form of public utterance, from mass media productions to old boy network speeches, was riddled with sexism of the most demeaning kind. Little or none of this was publicly acknowledged or admitted. If it was, women usually got the blame.

So it was hardly surprising that second wave feminism, emerging first in the United States and Britain, caught on quickly; nor that it was young, well educated Pakeha women, often married mothers, who took it up first. We were the group who had the resources—not money so much as education, mobility, a little spare time, and the confidence born of growing up in post-war prosperity—to stop and take note of what was happening to us and to other women, and start making a fuss about it publicly as well as personally. In 1973 *Broadsheet* asked women to say why they joined Auckland Women's Liberation. Giselle wrote,

> I joined the Movement because, as a wife, mother, housewife and woman I was seeing myself as a complete failure. I really started thinking seriously about our society and the roles we are expected to play. I could quite easily have played the game and been a wife and mother accepted by all, but this never would have made me happy. In fact, I think it would have driven me crazy.[1]

Later we found out that women had been there nearly a century before us, raising many of the same issues, often in remarkably similar terms. But they were forced to concentrate on one massive injustice, the denial of the vote to women. They were also much more constrained than we were by crippling notions of how women could or could not behave.

That is not to imply that feminism and feminists had vanished in the years between. The more we learned about our own hidden or forgotten past, the more we realised that, in Dale Spender's words, there had 'always been a women's movement'.[2] But the second wave also involved realising that women were not all the same, that gender was only one basis for oppression—and for some women not the most important one. Straight women learned how deeply homophobia was entrenched in New Zealand; Pakeha women learned what monoculturalism and racism did to Maori.

If we had known our own history better, both as women and as Pakeha, we would have made much faster progress. But as we soon came to realise, *not* knowing our own history was part of the problem.

Feminists didn't come out of nowhere, nor did we emerge simply in reaction to what we suddenly perceived to be the evils of an unchanging status quo. Deep changes were already occurring in areas as apparently unconnected as the export market and family patterns. These clashed with unchanged, die-hard assumptions about the only 'right' way to live and work, and blanket condemnations of those who didn't conform—such as mothers who put their children in daycare centres, or wanted a career.

Feminism was one of the responses to the contradictions and tensions of those times.

As feminists brought into the open issues such as suburban neurosis, workplace discrimination and harassment, family violence, and the problems faced by Maori and lesbian women, we got the blame for inventing or causing these so-called private problems. At the same time, feminists were quickly characterised, especially by the media, as that arrogant lot putting down the silent majority of ordinary women who were 'just housewives', and wanting to push them all out into paid jobs.

But women had already begun to move, by choice and necessity, out of their homes and into the labour market. By the seventies this movement was speeding up, as more and more of the old barriers which kept married women out of paid work came down. Not getting pregnant if we didn't want to was easier than ever before. Home appliances were rapidly altering the shape of housework. Although it was still Mum who ran the automatic washing machine, it was certainly easier than fishing sheets out of a copper and forcing them through a wringer. Not keeping the tins full of fresh home baking, or failing to provide three solid home cooked meals a day, was no longer a sin. And thanks to the urgent need for teachers and nurses in the baby boom years, even leaving pre-schoolers with someone else was starting to be less of a crime and easier to arrange.

Feminists have consistently emphasised both sides of the coin. We battled constantly to get the labour market to change in ways which would make it easier for women to join it and prosper in it. But that didn't mean devaluing the unpaid work women were doing—just the opposite. Feminists argued that managing a household budget should count for as much on a cv as doing the same work in an office. Bringing up children was developing human resources; running the local playcentre was management experience. But that was just the start. Getting the value of women's unpaid work recognised had to go hand in hand with improving conditions on the home job front, and sharing the load more equitably with men and with the state.

Being New Zealanders, feminists turned to the state, both as enemy and as ally. We understood that despite its claim to be a welfare state, it was heavily implicated in perpetuating the structures which kept women oppressed, from an education system which reinforced sexist stereotypes and kept female workers in the lowest ranks, to a tax system which advantaged male breadwinners, and a legal system which condoned domestic violence.

But we also understood that the state was not inherently oppressive. It could help women when it chose (or was forced) to do so. In 1911 it had brought in a widows' benefit; in 1973 it brought in the Domestic Purposes Benefit, making it possible for single, deserted, abused or thoroughly unhappy mothers to survive as sole parents. We might oppose a great deal of what the state did and how it did it—such as snooping on sole mothers to make sure they didn't have a man on the side—but we firmly believed that we could influence it for the better. In such a small society, where most people went through the state education system, we saw those who ran the state and made the decisions on our behalf as—apart from being almost all men—essentially no different from us, rather than as a remote elite.

So New Zealand feminism strongly emphasised transforming the state, in order to make it more representative of the community as a whole. We believed this was both feasible and essential. How else could we bring about real change for all women? The state provided essential services, employed large numbers of women, could be influenced by democratic organisation, and had the power to require other sectors to change how they treated women.

The Matrimonial Property Act 1976, which assumed a 50/50 entitlement to family property when a couple divorced, regardless of financial contribution, is one example of feminism's impact; the Parental Leave Act 1987 is another. But we soon learned that legislative change was only a necessary first step, and could not in itself create equality. We also had to change how state agencies behaved—for example, how they dealt with such issues as domestic violence. We had to get a fair share of the state's resources for women. And above all we had to ensure that enough women took part in state decision-making, not only as elected representatives, officials and employees, but as those on the receiving end of the decisions.

By the eighties, the energy, enthusiasm and optimism of the

early years of the women's liberation movement were flagging. The recession had taken hold, and we were having to face up to how diverse women's lives were and how complex the problem was. We no longer expected to win so much so soon.

But we still believed that we would continue to move toward equality, and although most of the early, across-the-board groups ceased to operate, we found new ways to advance our cause. Feminism moved out of small groups and into the wider community. Church women began to challenge male domination of church decisions, hierarchies and language, and pushed for investigations of sexism. Women in the arts moved from demanding a fairer share of everything—history, gallery space, funding— to challenging the meaning of art itself, unleashing a flood of magnificent (and often strongly political) work by and about women. Feminist teachers and other women workers increasingly insisted that their unions and professional organisations fully represent their interests, and lobbied successfully for new positions and structures to give women members an effective voice. The first national black women's hui was held in 1980. The Maori women's movement quickly gathered strength and impact, spurred on by the Springbok tour and Bastion Point, and constantly challenged Pakeha feminists to understand and keep pace.

Against this background, Labour Party women, who had formed their own council in 1975, put together for the 1984 election one of the most comprehensive women's policies ever drawn up in this country. It covered early childhood care and education, job training and employment, 'social and cultural equality' for women working at home and in the community, equality in education, women's health, control of fertility (with a review of the grounds for abortion and the certifying consultants' system), and legal and political equality.

Much *has* changed since the early seventies. Women now take a visible part in public life as of right, as citizens, rather than as merely token women. A female governor general, bishop, or Minister of Finance was almost unthinkable 20 years ago. None of the present incumbents would be where they are today if it hadn't been for feminism—though that does not mean they are all feminists now. And it certainly doesn't mean, as the media are so fond of trumpeting, that women have made it and don't need feminism any more.

Virtually all instances of legal discrimination, except for participation in the armed forces, have been removed from our statutes. The public tone has begun to alter, so that women are no longer constantly faced with stereotyped language and images which routinely put them down and treat them as a ridiculous, incompetent subspecies, or place them on equally ridiculous pedestals, ruthlessly attacking them when they fall off.

The worst aspects of men's power that women once had to cope with alone and in private—domestic violence, sexual harassment and abuse of all kinds, including incest—are now publicly recognised as endemic, serious and wrong. The blame is beginning to be laid not on male hormones, booze, or even the way some 'sick' men abuse their power over women, but on what feminists have long insisted is the basic cause: the way men in general are persistently trained to hold and exercise such power. The latest report on the justice system and domestic violence makes the next step plain: to put women's safety first and get the message on violence across, stop asking why he did it, just stop him doing it again.

The once so sharp distinction between married and unmarried motherhood—or rather married or unmarried consenting heterosexual activity—is now mercifully blunted. In the case of couples living together, it has virtually vanished altogether, doing away with an enormous amount of unnecessary shame and misery. There is broader, though by no means total, acceptance of sexuality other than heterosexuality, and discriminating against people because of their sexuality was made illegal in 1993.

Far more people, with and without children, now agree that parents need affordable, good quality child care, and that children benefit from pre-school programmes, which now involve 92 percent of all four-year-olds (though only 75 percent of Maori four-year-olds). Women working in kindergartens and child care centres, in voluntary organisations, trade unions, parliament, and the Labour Party, succeeded in getting this basic feminist issue onto the government's agenda. Anne Meade, a key figure in the campaign, described how they did it by placing 'a widely shared set of ideas and policy alternatives' in front of politicians, and then exerting 'fairly united pressure' to get them accepted.[3]

So many wives and mothers now go out to work for pay that society as a whole has stopped seeing this as a problem in itself, although individual women can still face family criticism, and a workload which includes almost all the housework. Despite massive increases in official unemployment figures, no one is insisting this time around, as they have in every other depression, that the solution is for married women to give up their jobs. For a brief time during 1990 it even seemed that real pay equity, including equal pay for work of equal value, was within reach.

Our faith in democracy was not entirely misplaced. Feminism, combined with social change, did succeed in forcing the state to shift its traditional approach to such issues—even to the extent of establishing a Ministry of Women's Affairs, whose staff have, by and large, continued to come up with advice, arguments and (when they have the money) projects in line with broad feminist principles.

Today politicians don't openly attack broadly accepted feminist goals: the National government has not abolished the Ministry of Women's Affairs, and it went to some trouble to explain that it was repealing the Employment Equity Act 1990, not because it was opposed to equity, but because it didn't believe the Act would achieve it. Instead, then Minister of Labour Bill Birch said in January 1991, they would 'implement specific policies to ensure that equal employment opportunities are addressed in the workplace'. Ominously, he went on to talk about how good the Employment Contracts Act 1991 would be for women and minority groups, because it encouraged 'flexibility'.[4]

As feminist ideas gained ground in New Zealand, the country's economic position was changing. Our focus as feminists had been mainly on the social realities—we had no significant response to the economic realities. Others did. In the second half of the eighties, with remarkable speed, new right philosophy swept New Zealand. Both Labour (from 1984 to 1990) and National (from 1990) governments pursued policies designed to promote private interests and success for the few, rather than the public interest and excellence for all. They set out to reduce taxes on the better off, turn state businesses into profit maximising state-owned enterprises or sell them off completely, separate funding from provision in major service areas such as health, turn universal entitlements into means tested privileges, and reduce state spending generally, especially where it 'distorted the market' or 'encouraged dependency'. They pushed 'consumer interests', rather than promoting real social and political power through participatory democracy. In place of collective responsibility, they isolated the individual and fostered powerlessness. Their values were the antithesis of those which had motivated and inspired the second wave of feminism.

Ironically, the most serious challenge to feminism has come not from those asserting the inferiority of women, or an inherently different female role, but from those who claim to value the individual and the individual's freedom above all else. In New Zealand, new right arguments were couched in carefully gender neutral language, and avoided overtly moralistic positions. They reduced men and women alike to 'labour units', 'consumers', 'taxpayers' and 'beneficiaries', and they co-opted many key aspects of the feminist critique of the welfare state, such as calls for increased accountability, 'flexibility' and 'choice'.

Although feminists had, quite properly, spent a lot of time and effort attacking what we saw as the deficiencies of the welfare state for women, we had not questioned its most basic premise—that the state could, and should, use the resources available to it to improve the lives of its citizens. Indeed, much of what we were doing depended utterly on that premise.

It is no coincidence that just when we were starting to get real results, and the state was beginning to open up to women, Maori and other groups, new right policies began shifting major areas out of reach or taking them entirely out of the state's domain.

By 1985 most of the early broad, all-purpose feminist groups had disappeared and been replaced by special interest groups focusing on specific issues—health, education, child care, violence against women, the growing problem of pornography. These groups were the only ones doing much of the longer-term work on key feminist goals, and they could tackle only one at a time. As the recession deepened and the new right gained ground, more and more women needed their help: they had to run faster and faster just to stay in the same place. Within the ranks of feminists, many now in full-time employment or themselves struggling to survive, there seemed to be a widespread move away from organising and taking action around policy goals, towards a focus on individual women achieving and moving up whatever ladder they could find—though many did their best to promote feminist goals along the way.

The nineties finally ended any illusions about continuing progress for women in general. Between 1987 and 1992, unemployment tripled in the female labour force as a whole, going from 3.9 to 9.4 percent. For Maori women, it doubled from a much higher base of 11.1 percent to a staggering 21.8 percent—over one in five Maori women were unemployed.[5] By 1992 one family in four had a sole parent, and over 80 percent of these families, compared with less than 18 percent of two parent families, reported an income of less than $15,000. The growth of unemployment was obvious in the growing proportion of sole parent families who had to rely on a benefit: between 1976 and 1991, it rose from 60 to 84 percent.[6] Sole parents are almost all women, as are the majority of those on benefits. Women and children are the two largest groups adversely affected by changes to welfare provisions, including accident compensation.

The Employment Contracts Act 1991 has had a severe impact on low paid women scattered in thousands of small workplaces. It is they who, as Linda Hill wrote in *Broadsheet*, are being 'decollectivised, deunionised and made invisible'. Since the Depression of the thirties, when 'both employers and workers were caught in a downward spiral of undercutting on wages', it has been acknowledged that the only way to protect them was through a national award. As more areas of the public sector are forced to fit a so-called market model, with 'funders' contracting 'providers' for a set term, even skilled women such as nurses 'may soon be in the same position as women working for commercial cleaning companies: their job security will only be as good as the term of the [provider's] contract'.[7]

The Employment Contracts Act has also made it impossible to find out exactly what is happening to women workers. Linda Hill points out that most New Zealand enterprises employ fewer than 12 people and, outside teaching and nursing, most women's jobs are in these small workplaces. But only collective contracts for more than 20 people need to be lodged with the Department of Labour, and even then they are unobtainable under the Official Information Act 1982.[8]

'Pessimism', Marina Warner writes, 'tends to leave the status quo in place, and works to stabilize the topsy-turvy. It consequently suits men in power, however harshly the powerful might be portrayed.'[9] The past eight years have taught us that economic policy can completely pre-empt social policy options.

But although feminists did not come to grips with some aspects of economic change, we did thoroughly understand others —and these may prove to be the most important. Even the Organisation for Economic Co-operation and Development (OECD) has begun to take in what we have been insisting all along: that economies, and societies as a whole, depend as much on their unpaid as on their paid workers. A 1992 OECD report stated quite bluntly:

> An efficient household and community sector is the foundation of an efficient productive sector and benefits society as a whole ... Improving the conditions under which unpaid 'non-market' activities are carried out might help avoid a crisis in household production and community care.[10]

It listed measures which might support unpaid workers—leave, expenses, training, access to social protection. It pointed out (again, echoing feminists) that anti-discrimination and equal opportunity programmes 'have not tackled head-on the systematic nature of inequality in employment'. The report came to much the same conclusion as the Royal Commission on Social Policy in 1988: that the relationship between paid and unpaid work, who does it and under what conditions, is at the heart of continuing inequalities between men and women, here as elsewhere.

Second wave feminists got bogged down in the old dilemma that beset all our predecessors: some of our arguments seemed to be based on the idea that women were or ought to be exactly the same as men, and others on assuming that we were completely different. But as most of us knew, and as new right policies have clearly revealed, neither are true—and neither work as models for organising society. We have to shift the focus so that men stop being seen as an unchangeable given, the current male pattern of work stops being defined as the norm, and women are no longer expected to resolve the tension between market and home, between paid and unpaid work.

The current New Zealand mix of deregulating, reshaping the labour market and cutting welfare, combined with high unemployment, is moving society in exactly the opposite direction to this. The new right approach places all the value on the paid work and none on unpaid, just as it places all the emphasis (in theory) on refusing to treat women differently in any way, and calls this equality.

The heartening thing is that most New Zealanders—and certainly most women—believe this is the wrong direction. They are not convinced that the benefits of new right policies will trickle down to them in the short-term, the medium-term, or ever. They persist in believing that the state ought to be their friend; and they do not agree that the ordinary citizen should expect no more effective say in how the country or its essential services are run than a minor shareholder in a multinational company. In short, they stubbornly refuse to accept that what's good for the Business Roundtable and the multinationals is good for New Zealand.

On the whole, New Zealanders have proved much more willing to accept feminist arguments than new right arguments. As the economic situation forces more and more people to move away from their old patterns and think of new ways of surviving, feminists are starting to develop a new economic analysis. It will be one that reflects the realities of women's lives as well as men's, and it will look for solutions which involve and serve the many, not the few. Its performance will be judged by new measures, which will include unpaid work and effects on the environment.

New Zealand is a small community and many levers of power are still within our reach. But a change of direction will not come unless feminists organise again on a massive scale. Through our unions in the workplace—which is why the right to organise is crucial—and through our groups and bases in the community, we can revitalise the concept of real equality, and reclaim democracy and the state as the ultimate expression of our collective responsibility for each other.

One small step in the meantime would be a requirement for all Treasury and Reserve Bank officials, judges and company directors to spend three months of every year working in early childhood centres or rest homes, or as cleaners or full-time housekeepers for young families. The effect on the quality of their decisions and advice would be miraculous.

Notes

1 'True Confessions: Why I joined Auckland Women's Liberation'. In *Broadsheet* No. 11, July 1973, pp 9–10

2 Dale Spender, *There's Always Been a Women's Movement*. Pandora Press, Boston 1983

3 Anne Meade, 'Women and Young Children Gain a Foot in the Door'. In *Women's Studies Journal* Vol. 6, Nos 1/2, November 1990, pp 96–110

4 Bill Birch, 'Why the repealed Act offered no employment and no equity'. *The Evening Post*, 22 January 1991

5 'MWWL and Te Puni Kokiri working together'. *Te Puni Kokiri Newsletter*, No. 1, June 1992

6 'One parent families now 1 in 4'. *The Dominion*, 2 May 1992

7 Linda Hill, 'The Budget Blues or How Economics Make Women Disappear'. *Broadsheet* No. 195, September 1992, pp 39–43

8 Linda Hill, 1992

9 Marina Warner, 'The Cricket's Song'. In *Times Literary Supplement*, 4 October 1991, p 4

10 'Shaping Structural Change: The Role of Women'. OECD report, Paris, 1992

Donna Awatere Huata is Ngati Whakaue, Ngati Porou. The author of *Maori Sovereignty*, she is a veteran activist for Treaty of Waitangi issues and Maori women's issues, and a director of Ihi Communications and Consultancy. She lives in Hastings, is married to Wi Huata, and has six children ranging in age from 22 years to six months.

Phillida Bunkle teaches Women's Studies at Victoria University, and is well known for her shrewd and brilliant feminist analyses of economics, politics and health. Her books include *Women in New Zealand Society* and *Second Opinion: the politics of women's health in New Zealand*. She joined the Alliance in 1992 and was selected as Ohariu candidate for the 1993 election. She has two teenage children, Jesse and Hester.

Sandra Coney, writer, health activist and an editor for 14 years of *Broadsheet*, has spent the past five years compiling a social history of New Zealand women, *Standing in the Sunshine*. She is also the author of five books, including *Every Girl: A Social History of Women and the YWCA* and *Out of the Frying Pan*, a collection of her columns from the *Dominion Sunday Times* and other writings. Her article with Phillida Bunkle, 'The Unfortunate Experiment', led to the setting up of the Cartwright Inquiry into cervical cancer treatment at National Women's Hospital.

Sonja Davies entered the New Zealand parliament as a Labour MP in 1987 after a pioneering career in the trade union movement, where she was the first woman to be vice president of the Federation of Labour. She wrote about her extraordinary life as unionist, feminist, child care advocate and peace worker, and her long battle with tuberculosis, in her autobiography *Bread and Roses*, published in 1985 and now a major television series.

Anne Else helped found *Broadsheet* in 1972 and has been writing and publishing about women ever since. From 1988 to 1991 she edited the *Women's Studies Journal*. In 1989 with Heather Roberts she co-edited the anthology *A Woman's Life*, and in 1991 published *A Question of Adoption*. Her most recent project, *Women Together*, a history of women's organisations, has been published by Daphne Brasell Associates Press and the Historical Branch of the Department of Internal Affairs to mark the centenary of women's suffrage in 1993.

Sue Kedgley, a freelance journalist and Wellington city councillor for the Green party, co-authored New Zealand's first feminist book of the 'second wave', *Sexist Society*, in 1973. She has since explored male-female relationships in *The Sexual Wilderness* and the life stories of New Zealand women writers in *Our Own Country*. She lives in Wellington with her husband, Dennis Foot, and three-year-old son Zachary, and is currently working on *Mum's the Word*, a history of motherhood.

Fiona Kidman began writing in her early twenties and has become one of New Zealand's most distinguished writers. She is the author of five novels, including *A Breed of Women*, published in 1979 and now recognised as a classic for its depiction of small town life and the struggle of a woman to find her own identity. Her most recent short story collection, *The Foreign Woman*, was published in 1993. Her extended family includes Joanna, Giles and Vannessa, and four grandchildren, Amelia, Zach, Toby and Reuben. She lives in Wellington with her husband Ian.

Rosslyn Noonan has been a university tutor, trade union secretary, member of the Royal Commission on Social Policy, writer, activist, full-time mother and Wellington city councillor. Presently secretary of the New Zealand Educational Institute, she is married to Michael Noonan and has two children, Matthew and Sarah.

Charmaine Pountney has been involved in trying to improve New Zealand's education system for 30 years. She has been on national committees for teaching, curriculum, examinations, and union affairs, represented New Zealand internationally, been principal of Auckland Girls' Grammar, Hamilton Teachers' College and, most recently, founding principal and dean of the School of Education at the University of Waikato. In 1992 she left institutional life to work with her partner Tanya Cumberland on a farm on the shores of the Manukau Harbour, where she has responsibility for pipes, fences, the hens and the herb garden.

Pat Rosier turned 50 in 1992 and, after 30 years in Auckland, emigrated with her partner to Nelson. The move brought to an end a seven years association with *Broadsheet*, as a collective member and editor. Her book *Been Around for Quite a While*, a selection of articles from twenty years of *Broadsheet*, was published in 1992. A former Women's Studies tutor and group facilitator for Auckland WEA, she is continuing this work, and her own writing, in Nelson.

Dame Mira Szaszy was New Zealand's first Maori woman university graduate. As national secretary of the Maori Women's Welfare League and later its president, she consistently urged greater rights for Maori women, including the right to speak on marae. Now retired from her profession as Maori Studies lecturer, and living in rural Kaitaia, she recently spent two years travelling New Zealand recording the stories of foundation members of the League for a new book, *Te Timatanga—Tatau Tatau*. She is a vice patron of the 1993 Suffrage Centennial Year Trust, Whakatu Wahine.

Mary Varnham is a freelance journalist and columnist for *The Evening Post*, where her incurable feminist views have agitated government ministers, glossy Auckland journalists, television bosses and fellow columnists. Convener of Media Women from 1986 to 1989, she has written and spoken extensively on women's issues. She is presently writing a history of the girls' school she attended, Woodford House, and compiling oral histories of women in the media. She lives in Wellington with her husband, Paul O'Regan, and children Christopher, Sylvia and Ciaran.

Allison Webber worked for Television New Zealand in its heyday of women's programming and made the pioneering series *Expressions of Sexuality*, which TVNZ withheld for years as too hot to show. A longtime media teacher and former head of the Wellington Polytechnic School of Journalism, she has been a leading advocate of greater rights and visibility for women and Maori in the media. She and her husband, John Anderson, run their own film company, Endeavour Productions, and live at Paekakariki with their daughter Lucy.